YOU MIGHT ⟨✓⟩ **W9-CGK-754**
THINKING IT
BY THE TIME YOU FINISH IT,
YOU WILL REALIZE IT IS ABOUT
HOW MUCH IN LIFE THERE IS TO SEE.

"The one pure and unencumbered sensation after
reading this book is the understanding that
being blind is not necessarily a limitation. Sullivan
is more than blind, or muscular, or a good singer.
He is a human being with positive things to
add to his life and to those he touches . . .
a series of consciousness-raising events awaits
you."—CHICAGO TRIBUNE BOOK WORLD

"Tom Sullivan reaches out from his own darkness
into the lives of the sighted to reveal a great
understanding of both worlds. From a child
sitting isolated in a fenced yard, to a student at
Harvard and his loneliest moments . . .
Sullivan grew to be a warm, fulfilled person . . .
If you could only see what he hears, life could
hold many more rewards."—SACRAMENTO BEE

"A frank story, an inspirational story . . . a
testament to man's ability to survive—and to
conquer—adversity."—RICHMOND NEWS-LEADER

IF YOU COULD
SEE WHAT
I HEAR

BY
Tom Sullivan
AND
Derek Gill

A SIGNET BOOK
NEW AMERICAN LIBRARY
TIMES MIRROR

This is an authorized reprint of a hardcover edition published by Harper & Row, Publishers, Inc. The hardcover edition was published simultaneously in Canada by Fitzhenry & Whiteside Limited, Toronto.

Insert photos pp. 1-4, Frank McGee.
Movie photos courtesy Jensen-Farley Pictures, Inc.

SIGNET TRADEMARK REG. U.S. PAT. OFF. AND FOREIGN COUNTRIES
REGISTERED TRADEMARK—MARCA REGISTRADA
HECHO EN CHICAGO, U.S.A.

SIGNET, SIGNET CLASSICS, MENTOR, PLUME, MERIDIAN AND NAL BOOKS *are published by The New American Library, Inc., 1633 Broadway, New York, New York 10019*

FIRST SIGNET PRINTING, JULY, 1976

13   14   15   16   17   18   19

PRINTED IN THE UNITED STATES OF AMERICA

Contents

Author's Note

I am blind. But the message I hope to convey in this book is that the joy of living life to the full has far out-weighed the inconvenience of my physical handicap. I trust my story will encourage the reader to strive for his personal goals, whatever the obstacles, and will provide some inspiration by example. It has not been easy for me, a skeptic, to advance this optimistic prospect. That I have is due to a great number of people. The names of some of them will be found in the chapters that follow. Most of the names are real ones, but where embarrass-ment is likely to be caused, I have used pseudonyms and certain other disguises.

I would mention particularly my father and mother, who cared for me enough to allow me to enter a world perhaps beyond their reckoning, and my wife, Patricia, and our children, who have helped me scale the peaks of joy through the sharing of their love. Just as energy begets energy, so, I have discovered, love begets love.

I would like to thank Derek Gill, who "became" Tom Sullivan. Through his pen I gained a deeper understand-ing of my feelings, motivations and aspirations. He showed me a brighter horizon than I had previously acknowledged, and in bringing my life story into focus he helped me see purpose and meaning in my life.

Beyond being a story of striving, this book may also be seen as a testament to youth, because it seems to have evolved into a youthful quest for truth.

1. The Breath of Life

Blythe reached for my hand and started tugging. Then the phone rang. "Come, Daddy, swim," she was saying with the impatience of a three-year-old.

I was tempted to ignore the phone. The June sun was warm, the pool seductive, the California air heady with mock orange blossom. Patty, my wife, had gone to pick up groceries at the supermarket.

But the phone went on ringing imperiously. It is hard to allow a phone to ring for more than thirty seconds.

"Look, Blythe," I said. "I'm going to have to answer it. You just sit still on the step a moment." I circled the hot tiles around the pool and picked up the extension line.

The cultivated voice of an executive secretary said, "Mr. Sullivan? This is MGM. The president will be able to see you at four o'clock on Tuesday. Is that convenient?"

Convenient! I had been waiting two months for this appointment. Five A.M. on Sunday would have been convenient!

"Yes, that'll be fine," I said coolly.

"And would you please bring the test pressing of your new single," said the mid-Atlantic voice.

"I'll do that," I replied.

"There'll be an admission pass at the studio gate and you will be told where to park."

"I understand," I said.

Adrenaline was shooting my pulse up to a hundred. Oh, God, how long would Patty be? She had been waiting for this call as anxiously as I.

"Very well," said the secretary. "The president is looking forward to meeting you."

"Thank you," I said.

It was then that I heard the splash; not a loud one, just a splash like someone dropping a small stone into water. I wasn't alarmed. Blythe had probably thrown her life preserver into the pool. I replaced the receiver and called her name.

Silence.

"Blythe? Blythe?"

Beyond the hedge a truck was rumbling down the road. The excitement of the phone call from MGM went into a slow fade. Blythe had to be there somewhere. She was probably frightened by the concern in my voice. The tiles were uncomfortably hot. I stood on the outer edges of my feet.

"Blythe?" I called more gently. "It's okay. Daddy's not mad at you."

No response.

The significance of the splash began to impinge on my mind. I took three paces toward the step and tripped on the life preserver.

"Blythe? Blythe?" My voice, hard now, was touching the edge of fear.

The only sound was the murmur of the pool's filter. A moment more, and I was convinced she had fallen in. For the first time in my life I felt utterly helpless. For the first time in my twenty-six years I saw myself as others see a blind person—pathetically inadequate in facing a crisis like this. Reason warred with panic. If my daughter was drowning, it was useless to simply stand on the side of the pool. I jumped in, thrashing the water, yelling her name.

It may be true that when people are drowning they see their lives unraveling like a film. In this case it was I who experienced the phenomenon as the high points of Blythe's thirty-eight months of life flashed through my mind in staccato memories. I recalled the joy of her birth, the moment when her hand circled my forefinger, the smell of a newly bathed baby, the silk texture of her blond pigtails, the lisping of her first words, the warmth of her hug.

As the kaleidoscope of sounds, scents and touch completed its cycle, my mind searched, then hovered over a boyhood memory of discovering how, when playing in a pool, I could mark the position of an adversary by listening for bubbles.

I stopped thrashing the water and remained absolutely still. Then, very faintly, I heard a *Blip! Blip!* These had to be the sounds of life. I swam toward the bubbles and paused. *Blip! Blip!* Louder now. I dived under the surface, sweeping the bottom with my hands. It was my foot that touched her.

Scooping up the small body and breaking the surface, I called her name again. The only sound was the raindrop drip of water from her head, lolling over my forearm.

I pressed my daughter's thin ribs, expelling water from her chest. Then I began to breathe into her mouth—slowly, rhythmically. I was conscious of a pulse in her neck, soft as the fluttering of a fledgling.

Though physicists claim that seconds are evenly spaced, I can swear that some seconds stretch out and out into lapses of time unrelated to the pendulum swing of a grandfather clock. So it was now, with seconds ticking off in the slowest motion. I continued to breathe into the petal mouth, feeling the surge of air swell the fragile cage under my hands and then ease back. My mind was crying her name—and God's too: not a formed prayer, simply a yearning, a pleading for aid.

After how long I could not guess—three minutes, perhaps, or even five—I heard the sweetest sound that has ever reached my ears. It was a sound like a dove far away in the woods—a long-drawn *Coooh*. Twice she made this sound, the gentlest whisper of a human being reaching for life.

So Blythe began to breathe again. My own tears blinked her eyes awake after her journey into the mystery of death.

She sits beside me now as I tell my story. She has grown an inch or two. I can hear the squeak of her crayons across a sheet of paper. She may be trying to sketch her father. I won't know unless she tells me. I am not able to guide her hand or praise her effort to blend color or to capture form.

Blythe knows that. She understands. She seeks nothing of me but my love and she freely gives her own to the one who fathered her.

When saying good night to me last evening, she suddenly flung back the blanket and threw her arms about my neck.

"Was I lost, Daddy?" she asked.

I must have frowned as I tried to put context to the question.

"When I fell into the pool," explained Blythe.

"Ah, yes!" I exclaimed. "You were lost for a while."

"It was very dark—like *you* see things, Daddy."

I thought about this a moment and then said, "Oh, Blythe, if you could only see what I can hear."

I'm not sure she understood. Yet children understand more than we give them credit for. Anyway, she hugged me and said, "I love you, Daddy."

There are occasions when you can't say anything. This was such. In a comparatively short life of high adventure, dark fear, bitter frustration and perhaps more than my share of reward and happiness, last night's hug over a child's crib will always have its special meaning for me.

For just as Blythe did from the side of the pool, so I too reach out of the darkness for life.

2. Dawning and Darkness

I was born blind. At least that's what the record says; yet the record is not strictly true. When I fought my way out of the darkness of my mother's womb three months too early, I did in fact see the light of my first earth day. I weighed but four pounds, my life as fragile as gossamer. Had I been born a year or two earlier, the thread might have snapped within the hour and my parents might have spoken in nostalgic moments of the infant son whose cry they had heard before his heart had faltered and failed.

But in 1947 pediatrics had just taken a quantum jump. A human incubator, an artificial womb, had recently been invented, though not perfected. Through scientific ingenuity, premature babies previously doomed to die now survived. Quitting the warmth and security of my mother's body, I was placed inside a glass-sided box. Within my own environment, like an astronaut in a space capsule, a thermostat maintained the even warmth of my blood and a cylinder alongside the incubator fed oxygen to my lungs—too much oxygen.

That was the error. The doctors, the scientists, the nurses on twenty-four-hour duty at the Faulkner Hospital in West Roxbury, Massachusetts, did not then understand nature's delicate balance of air. Too little oxygen, and life and a candle flame die. Too much oxygen, and the lenses of my eyes began to mist like steam on a window. With a window, one can take a cloth and wipe away the misting. But not with eyes.

During those first years of the incubator, the medical world was puzzled that so many premature babies whose lives, like mine, had been saved by incubators were denied the gift of sight.

By the time medical science discovered the fault in the first incubators, ten thousand American babies had been plunged into lives of total darkness. When the cause of the blindness was discovered and corrected, a long name was given to the darkness that smothered the vision of premies. It was called retrolentalfibroplasia, which means the formation of a filament over the cornea of the eye that inhibits the penetration of light.

But my mother, resting in a bed in the maternity ward of the Faulkner Hospital, and my father, in a bar down the street, were ignorant of the snuffing out of their only son's miraculous cells of vision.

My mother, small-boned, blond and gentle, was praying to the Virgin to keep alive the flame and flicker of my life. My father, rambunctious, strong, scarred from fistfights, was standing in his own barroom and roaring for a third, a fourth, a fifth round of drinks on the house. It was his bar, after all, his liquor, his hospitality, his son.

Porky Sullivan had waited fourteen years for a son. Sure his son would survive. Had he not been given the blood of the Sullivans? Not Italian blood, not Jewish blood, but pure Boston Irish.

For sure the babe was small ... "But I'll wager a hundred bucks the son of a bitch'll one day lick the hide off Tussey Russell."

Within the next few weeks my father came perilously close to losing his first bet on my prowess. My weight dropped to three pounds and paused. The incubator bellows continued to wheeze over-oxygenated air into my lungs. The thermostat kept my temperature at 98.6 degrees Fahrenheit. Twice a day my mother, home now in our lace-curtain Irish suburb, drained the milk from her breasts, and twice a day my father carried the precious fluid to Faulkner Hospital. Slowly, very slowly, the wrinkled skin around my bones began to stretch as the tissues of my body absorbed maternal nourishment.

So the baby Thomas Sullivan, mewling and kicking, was released from the hospital and taken home, there to be cooed over by relatives, including his sisters, Peggy and Jean, and by neighbors.

Dad did not coo. He was too masculine for soft noises of approval. He laughed and rumbled as he lifted me above his head and felt the firming of my limbs. "The kid knows me already," he boasted to my grandmother. To prove that I could perceive movement, he brought a flashlight to my crib and beamed it over my face. But when my eyes did not follow the light his laughter faded.

This was the moment when concern was first voiced about my vision. Oddly out of character, my father, not my mother, proposed taking me to a neighborhood doctor to check the lack of response in my pupils. I was four months old.

After the doctor had examined me, he turned to my parents and said all too bluntly, "Your son is blind."

Had the doctor hit my father across the face with his stethoscope, he could not have been more stunned and stung. After a moment he shouted, "You lying bastard. He's not blind! He'll see! He'll see! My son will see!" Thus shouting, Dad turned about and charged through the doctor's crowded reception room, into the street. Mom took me home—and wept.

Dad vanished for five days. Friends and family made inquiries. There was not a bar within miles of home that Dad had not visited. Mom eventually sent out one of Dad's barmen to track him down. His fury was spent but he still refused to accept my blindness as permanent. Over the next twelve months Dad took me from doctor to doctor. Opthalmologists from Boston to New York pronounced the same verdict. "Your son will not see again."

Only when there were no more doctors on his list and no more to be recommended did he accept the fact; then, assailed by guilt, he would protest to Mom that he was responsible. Had he not gone on a wild weekend to Florida with his Irish friends the week before I was born? If he had stayed at home, would my mother have carried the child full term? Was the blindness of his son some sort of Providential punishment for his prodigality? When his soul-searching and sense of guilt began to ease, Dad threw his enormous energy and enthusiasm into creating a Parents of the Blind organization—a sort of Alcoholics Anonymous to encourage parents of blind children to meet together to discuss their common problems. Over the next years Dad personally raised many thousands of dollars for the blind. As for his relationship with me, far from rejecting his blind son, he garnered all the love of which he was capable and focused it on me.

In my first two or three years I was, of course, totally unaware of the emotional family drama created by my blindness. I did not know what blindness was, simply because I did not know the meaning of sight.

Looking back over the years, my first deep-etched memory is of loneliness, of isolation from other children, except from my sister Peggy, seven years older than I and my constant baby-sitter.

When Peggy went to school, Mom put me out in the fenced backyard of our suburban home. I recall the touch of grass in that yard and the texture of the dirt. A swing, rusted and squeaking, was the center of my universe. A vivid early memory is of the day I discovered that I could twist the swing and then, on its unraveling, be spun around at speed. Movement for the blind person is as important as the sweep of eyes for a sighted person. This is the reason many blind children, whether they are sitting or standing, are almost always rocking, always moving. A sighted person is constantly aware of motion—a curtain blowing in a breeze, a person walking across a room, someone shifting papers on a desk. When a blind person moves, he feels he is a participant in the action about him.

Unconsciously I was developing the peculiar attribute of facial vision—a kind of "radar" some blind people acquire. What this amounts to is a reflection of sound waves off the facial muscles. It is the same sense that is developed to a higher degree by bats and porpoises. When anyone moves, he cuts through air and sends out waves the way that a stone dropped into a pond sends out ripples. The different degree and intensity of the rebounding air hitting the face can tell the blind person not only that there is an object a short distance away but the rough dimensions of the object too. When I was much older I took part in scientific tests on this developed sensitivity. I was placed alone in the middle of a large empty parking lot where there were many telephone poles. By using facial vision, I was able to run around the lot without hitting a pole.

I see my first four years as the emptiest, if not the unhappiest, time of my life. There were to be later periods of deep frustration and vitriolic bitterness; but this was a period of bleak friendlessness. I spent endless hours alone swinging on my swing, waiting for attention. My mother, busy about her household chores, left me largely to my own resources in our yard. I measured time by sound—of schoolchildren breaking class for lunch, or a van delivering bagels to the delicatessen down the street, or my father shaving and washing.

Dad tackled even simple things like his ablutions with his characteristic extraordinary vigor. As a barkeeper, he kept late hours, and he slept each morning until ten. When he had shaved, he dipped his head

under the water in the bathroom basin and blew
bubbles about his ears—a sound that floated out to me
as a regular morning time check, giving me comfort
and a secure sense of my father's presence.

A high point of each day was the arrival in the late
afternoon of Fritzie, the paper boy. Though probably
no more than twelve, he had already developed a
degree of compassion; he never failed to play with me
for five minutes or so. He pushed the swing or gave me
rides on his back or wrestled me to the ground. If I
had any goal at all at this time, it was to grow as tall
and strong as Fritzie. When he continued on his paper
route, I wrestled with myself, often punching my face
until it was bruised.

There was some adventuring forth from the yard
with Peggy or my mother—usually to a park or to the
delicatessen, from which I would return sticky-handed
from a Popsicle or ice-cream cone. But these expeditions were even more boring than the yard. I could not,
like sighted kids, look at toys in store windows or at
fire engines in the street. With Mom I usually had to
stand still, my hand tugging at her skirt, and listen to
endless gossip with a neighbor about someone's illness
or to discussions of the price of cheese.

When she took me for walks, Mom presumed she
was giving me treats. She could not understand my
whining reluctance. My most effective protest was to lie
on the floor and scream, but Mom soon found a coun-
termeasure: she invented a character called Mrs.
Wiggs, whose profession was the punishment of disobedient children. To create Mrs. Wiggs, Mom entered
into a conspiracy with Mrs. Sheehan next door. Mrs.
Sheehan sneaked into our cellar, and when I heard
slow, sinister steps, Mom hissed, "Mrs. Wiggs is
coming to get yer, Tommy."

If I still resisted, I heard the disguised, sepulchral
voice of Mrs. Wiggs declaring, "I'm coming, Tommy.

I'm coming to take you away." At this point resistance invariably collapsed.

In the 1940s and deep into the '50s, there was no community assistance for parents of blind children. Mom was convinced that her main task was to protect me from both the perils and the challenges of the sighted world. Most sighted children learn more from other children than they do from their parents. Aside from Peggy and Fritzie, who were more than twice my age, I have no memory of contact with other children until I was four years old.

Mom's method of basic training would be condemned today by every child psychologist. It was essentially a training by criticism. The word "don't" became as familiar as my name. She praised me occasionally, but always for the wrong things. I was a "good little boy" if I had clean hands; yet I loved playing with mud. I was a good little boy if I didn't mess up the toilet; but my ambition was to wee the way my father did—in the standing position. Finding it difficult to aim at the unseen bowl, I was reprimanded when I attempted the masculine stance. I was a good little boy if I sat by myself in the yard, when I longed for childish company. I was a good little boy if I didn't bother Mom with questions. Yet I desperately wanted to know what was making that whistle in a tree or why my hair was curly when Fritzie's was smooth.

When I cut my lip on half-open doors or tripped over a curb, Mom blamed herself. One day she returned from a store with a cowboy outfit a couple of sizes too large. The cuffs flopped about my ankles and in walking downstairs I tripped and fell, gashing my head on the banister. Weeping, Mom picked me up and passionately assured me that she would never allow me to hurt myself again. The cowboy outfit was put away on a high shelf. I would have been willing to shed pints of blood to be allowed to wear it once again.

In my fourth year, my grandmother was my principal storyteller. Believing as firmly in leprechauns as she did in rewards for saying her rosary, she wheezed forth fairy stories with rare dramatic conviction. One serialized story concerned two gallant characters called Beanie and Cecil, who sailed around the world doing good works in their ship *Lena*. A mortal enemy, Mr. Oooh, possessed no fewer than fifty-two million heads, each one alert to pull the good ship *Lena* to the ocean floor. For some reason I believed that the toilet bowl would give Mr. Oooh the opportunity to thrust up one of his heads and drag me to hidden depths. I was totally convinced that Mr. Oooh had designs on Tommy Sullivan.

The result of this phobia—and no phobia is more powerful than a child's—was that I held back the natural pressures on my bladder almost to the point of rupture. When the pressure was unbearable, I ran to the bathroom and released everything with a huge explosion. I was convinced that if I discharged both barrels at once I could at least hold the monster at bay!

One frightening evening I dashed to the toilet, not knowing until too late that my father had left the seat up. My screams coincided with my small backside's hitting cold water, which, to me, had to be the clammy claws of Mr. Oooh.

I did not know Grandmother was dying, even when her wheeze turned into a death rattle. Her last words to me were: "Remember, Tommy, I'll always be watching you." Deep into my teen-age years I was convinced that Grandmother's ghost was at my elbow—a conviction strengthened by my inheriting her bed in the Greaton Road home. Indeed, there were times when, after committing some misdemeanor, I distinctly heard her Irish voice warning me of the temperature of hell.

A Mrs. Doolittle played a minor role on or about my fourth birthday. She persuaded Mom that I needed the company of children and arranged to take me along with her own small children to a neighborhood nursery school. I found myself in a playground surrounded by kids my own age. I was the object of intense interest. Small fingers prodded me and touched my eyes. For the first time I realized that I was different from other kids, even unique in this company. Initially I was treated with a sense of awe, as if I were a strange animal that had wandered from the zoo. I most urgently desired to be fully assimilated—to play with toys, to catch a ball, to jump and run. On the third day I decided to join the stampede I heard around me. The grass was soft under my feet, the wind was in my hair. I went on running until I crashed into a tree.

Mom arrived to take me home. As she wiped the blood off my nose, she told me that I would not be going to the nursery school anymore. When my rage had ebbed, Mom explained, "You can't do the things that other children do. You'll never be like other children, Tommy."

It was like a sentence to life imprisonment when I was returned to the yard surrounded by its chain-link fence.

Stricken by my loneliness, Dad bought me a radio and showed me how to tune in to the different stations. Marconi could never have imagined the gift he gave to a four-year-old blind boy in West Roxbury. This was a world of sound and action, a world of cowboys and Indians, of cops and robbers, of duels fought with swords and pearl-handled .38s. My intimates now were the Cisco Kid, Tom Mix, Nick Carter, Hopalong Cassidy, the gangsters and agents of the FBI series. I helped Ma Perkins run her lumberyard and wandered abroad with Gene Autry and his horse, Champion. I walked hospital wards with Dr. Malone. I crouched with the Lone Ranger behind a desert rock when he caught Big Bad Bart in his rifle sights. I floated down the Mississippi with Huck Finn and Tom Sawyer long before I was five years old.

While the kids at the nursery school skipped rope or messed about with finger paints, my own world was filled with an exhilarating company who rode the fastest horses, shot the straightest arrows in Sherwood Forest, or sailed the seven seas in search of treasure. My external world—the only world that mattered—was almost entirely in my mind.

In the morning before anyone was up, I replayed the radio adventures over and over. I tried to capture the sounds myself and so discovered, for instance, that bottle caps make a noise indistinguishable from the jingle of silver spurs. By tapping my slippers on the floor or smacking my stomach or clapping my hollowed hands, I could recreate the sound of a horse galloping over the baked dirt of Arizona, across the wooden bridge at Pohick Creek or along the hard pavement of a turnpike.

With the radio's help, my imagination filled and the high tide of my early loneliness began to ebb. Yet its very ebbing left me with a craving for physical adventure. The back yard was too small for me now. Somewhere beyond that chain-link fence there was the real world, which I wanted to discover, and not at the end of the sticky, usually reluctant hand of Peggy or the impatient hand of my mother.

The day came when I found I could climb the fence. My heart pounding, I eased myself down on the other side—to freedom. I was still on familiar ground. I knew the way to the delicatessen—past the lamppost, over the curb (listen for traffic), across the street. I also knew that if I went to the delicatessen itself I would be instantly recognized and be sent back home. I was now out alone for the first time with no one to push or pull me. I soon found myself in a narrow alley, where I bumped into a garbage can. I lifted the lid,

felt around and discovered what were obviously doughnuts, rock hard, maybe, but none I had eaten or have
ever eaten since have tasted as good. I felt like Huck
Finn discovering a crab-apple tree down by the river.

The alley was full of fascination. I found two sheets
of glass. I had not held a pane of glass before. I felt its
cold smoothness and the sharpness of its edge and then
deliberately dropped it. The sound was glorious—a
plop and then, instantly, myriad tiny bells rang out. I
dropped the second pane of glass and relished the en-
core.

I was lost for two hours. The West Roxbury police
searched every street and yard within three miles of
home for the lost blind boy—every street, that is, except the alley behind the delicatessen. It was Fritzie
who found me and carried me home on his shoulders.

Worse than my parents' scolding when finally I got
home was the pain of a churning stomach. Those garbage doughnuts had cultured some powerful bacteria,
which kept me bombing Mr. Oooh most of the night.

But this first lone adventure into the world beyond
my home marked the point where the path of my over-
protected infant years met the road leading to
boyhood. Blind though I was, nothing was going to
stop my being a boy.

3. Summers of Content

The coastal town of Scituate, north of Cape Cod, was my Camelot. There in 1950 Dad took possession of a summer house with a huge porch. I spent the happiest days of my young life at Scituate and memory of them is filled with the sounds and smell of the sea, the bleat of the Minot lighthouse foghorn on misty mornings, the touch of warm sand and slippery kelp, the thrill of first deep friendships. Memory closes in on the friendships that tugged me away from the lonely drag of days in the yard at West Roxbury and into days of such excitement that I resented sleep.

My father's Irish friends suddenly swept my radio heroes off the stage of my mind. I identified each of them by voice, touch and smell—a belly laugh, a hairy arm, a whiskey breath.

On Sunday mornings after Mass, the big clapboard house with its porch seemed to accommodate every Massachusetts Irishman of any importance. Mom not only tolerated the invasion but fed the invaders. The local poultry farm and baker made special deliveries of eggs, bagels and doughnuts to satisfy the enormous appetites of prize fighters, bums, bartenders and former bootleggers, who sat shoulder to broad shoulder with policemen and politicians.

The serious business of the day had to wait until the toothpicks were out and the plates cleared from the porch table. The prime purpose of the Sunday gatherings seemed to be drinking and the boastful conversation that flowed from liquor-loosened tongues. Dad's friends began drinking early on Sunday afternoon, continued on Sunday night and sometimes into Monday morning. I think I remember more than one occasion when they drank through Tuesday.

At the head of the table was Dad, the original flimflam man, by turns boisterous, moody, jubilant, angry, always shouting for more bottles, drowning conversation with his laughter or by thumping the tabletop to gain attention. Both the company and the liquor were imported from his West Roxbury bar.

Among the regulars on the porch I had my favorites. Spike Henessy was one. Spike had been in jail for thirty-five of his fifty-seven years. He and Uncle Joe, both trailing cigar smoke, played hide-and-seek with me among the closets. Beansy Thornton and Jonesy Smith were on my special list, for sometimes they broke the porch circle and took me to a ball game at Fenway Park. They never paid for tickets and when challenged they would protest, "Whaddya goin' to do—kick a blind kid outta here?" So from the best seats in the park, Beansy and Jonesy gave me a running commentary on the Red Sox games.

Others who came to our porch on Sundays included Mayor John Hynes of Boston, Sonny McDonagh of the Governor's Council, occasionally former Governor Maurice Tobin himself.

Even as a five-year-old, I loved to stand behind the chair of Captain Francis Murphy, head of the Boston Police Department, and listen to his growls when Specksy O'Keith boasted (mendaciously perhaps) of his part in the previous month's bank robbery or of the robbery he planned for next week.

Mom, moving swiftly back and forth between the kitchen and the porch, pounced upon and summarily fined any guest who swore. The amount of the fine depended on the color of the word. The bills were pinned to a wall, and at the end of a drinking session Mom collected the money and took the wives out shopping for new clothes.

I was the mascot of these weekend gatherings. Slurring ever more sentimentally with the opening of each fresh bottle, the guests stuffed my pockets with dimes, quarters and occasionally crisp bills.

From time to time I sneaked out into the yard to show off my treasure to Peggy, who, taking advantage of my monetary ignorance, would split the spoils to her outrageous advantage.

It is hard to separate my Scituate summers. Was I five, six or seven when Dad called for a boxing match between myself and his friend Tussey Russell? Gloves were found and the whole company moved into the yard, there to circle Tussey and small Tom. I would feel a feather touch on my nose and would wildly pummel back, my fists flailing like the sails of a windmill. Once Tussey must have been bending down or looking north, because my small fist shot out and connected with his jaw. The old champion of the ring rolled in the dirt. From the circle of Dad's friends there rose such a thunder of applause that it threatened to bring down the porch roof.

Then Dad's huge hands grasped me around the waist and he lifted me high above his head. He was my giant, both physically and heroically, and I was raised so high that I had to be somewhere near the moon. Height and depth were beyond my comprehension. A skyscraper elevator gave me no sense of ascending and I was often terrified when standing on a rock or ledge just a few inches above the ground. But when my father lifted me up I was thrilled beyond imagining, for his arms were strong and totally trustworthy.

"There, didn't I tell yer," thundered Dad. "My son's the champ."

I cherished Dad's friends—the barflies, the hellions, the politicians and policemen—and they all seemed to love me. None had a bigger heart than Tom McDonagh, then head of the Internal Revenue Department for the state. He introduced me to fishing, relishing the art no less than Izaak Walton. Dad accompanied us on our first expedition to the banks of the North River. I could sense anxiety in both men when, after an hour or so, not a nibble had bent the tip of my pole. Meanwhile Dad and old Tom had caught half a dozen flounders. I heard the two men whispering together and then Dad wading into the water. Suddenly I felt a throb on my line. I squealed with delight as I reeled in a twice-caught flounder. Many expeditions later, Tom McDonagh confessed how my first catch had been contrived.

But I had tasted a new sport, and twice a week through the long summers of my early youth Tom McDonagh picked me up at home and took me to the water.

Tom also taught me how to sail a boat, how to gauge the strain of rope, to understand the wind. He introduced me to the joy of feeling bow spray on my face. Sometimes he would talk but more often we were silent. I delighted in the company of this man who loved the sea, tight fishing lines, the groan of bottom boards, the flap of sails and the whoosh of brine in gunwales.

We were out in his boat one evening when a thick fog suddenly smothered us. For me the fog was simply an awareness of dampness and cold discomfort, and I was puzzled when Tom suddenly dropped the sails and said, "We're going to be late home tonight, son. I can't see a thing."

"I'm cold," I protested. "I want to go home."

Tom put his heavy coat over my shoulders and explained that he didn't know where he was and that it would be dangerous to sail until the fog had lifted. I tried to fathom his problem and then suggested, "Why don't you sail in the direction of the lighthouse?"

"I can't see the light," said Tom.

"But you can hear it," I replied, referring to the fog-horn.

Old Tom suddenly became uncharacteristically animated. "D'ya think you could guide us home, Tommy?"

For the first time in my life I was aware of being able to do something useful and special, something that even a wise, grown-up person like Tom McDonagh couldn't do. It seemed totally natural to me to point the boat toward the foghorn.

I sat on the bow and Tom raised the jib. The bleat of the Minot lighthouse gave me a precise course and, guided by the sound, I shouted the left or right instructions to the man at the tiller. We made the harbor without mishap, and I was bloated with pride when Tim recounted our experience to Dad. "We'd still be out there without that boy of yours," said Tom.

It was at Scituate that I made my first friendship with boys my own age. The encounter came about through a bad bargain. I was standing in front of our house with an air gun, a new toy. I heard short light steps coming down the street and then the salutation "Hi!" The boy came up and fondled my gun.

"Trade ya?" he asked.

"For what?" I replied cautiously, recalling some poor trades with sister Peggy.

"This," he said, pushing into my hands a rubber horseshoe. I had no idea what it was, but to plead ignorance would have been to lose status. The horseshoe felt interesting as I flexed it in my fists. "Okay," I said offhandedly, and he grabbed my gun before I could change my mind.

Now that the deal was made, we exchanged names, and a few minutes later we were joined by another boy, who sounded exactly like the first. That was natural, for John and David Turnbull were twins.

Although I gained their friendship with a bargain as

bad as any made in an Oriental bazaar, I had no cause to regret it, for John, David and I became close in hand, heart and adventure. It was John and David who introduced me to the thrill of climbing trees. It was they who, in our third Scituate summer, dared me to explore the spook house down the street.

The house, an old clapboard rambling place, had stood empty long enough to earn the reputation of being haunted. The twins and even older children would never have ventured down the weed-covered path and opened the creaking gate. I forget what spook was reputed to be its occupant, and indeed I found it hard to understand how a semivisible man would behave if I met him. For me everybody was invisible, so I felt I had the edge on those who could be terrified by shroud and jangling chains. I cannot, then, honestly boast about precocious courage when I announced to my awe-struck friends that Tommy Sullivan would find the ghost.

John and David guided me to the door, which opened to a penknife and a push. They left me, though, as I walked down protesting floorboards asthma-thick with dust, and so into the gloom of the inner rooms. Perhaps to scare the ghost or to give me fortitude, either Dave or Johnny smashed a window with a rock. All this accomplished was to alert a neighbor, who telephoned the police. By the time they arrived, I had met no spirit, blithe or vile. The twins had disappeared, leaving me to face the law alone. The officers bundled me into their patrol car and took me to the station. I listened with subjective interest to the altercation at the sergeant's desk.

"What in hell are the papers going to say when they hear we've pulled in a blind kid?" The question hung in the air until the sergeant gruffly asked my telephone number. Learning I was in jail, my father instructed the police to cool me in a cell for a couple of hours. I

now whether I hold a recordable achievement
haps worthy of the *Guinness Book of World
Records*, for I doubt whether any other six-year-old
blind boy has heard the clang of a steel door and found
himself incarcerated in a Massachusetts cell.

When Dad came for me two hours later, I sensed in-
sincerity behind his stern rebuke. A son of his who had
been in jail was considered, possibly, worthy of the hel-
lion company he kept.

Dad's character was the strangest mixture of
gentleness and ferocity. Sometimes he played with me
for hours and with infinite patience, as when he taught
me a modified game of baseball. He had a bat specially
made, just twenty inches long and thin enough at the
handle to allow my grip. He pitched experimentally, at
first rolling a volleyball at me along the dirt. When this
proved ineffective or too tame, he began to bounce the
ball several times and I would listen to its approach
and smite, completely missing nine times out of ten.
Then he tried a one-bounce pitch, with success at my
second and third strike.

"Pitch!" he bellowed, and then I listened for the
bounce two yards ahead of my feet. Here was the
signal for me to swing the bat. My stomach knotted
with excitement as I made contact and heard the ball
spinning down the dirt. The game became more and
more refined, and soon he had a first base marked out
and a scorecard too.

What delighted me was that John and David and the
other kids around the block came to join the Sullivan
baseball game, seemingly preferring it to their own.
They played with me not condescendingly, not merely
to keep company with a blind boy, but because they
genuinely preferred Sullivan baseball to the standard
rules. In the languid Scituate summers I began to find a
place of equality with my sighted peers.

From Scituate Dad commuted to his bar in West

Roxbury. He did not return every night, but it was always a joy for me to wake up and find that he was at home because I knew he would encourage me to play some new game or participate in a fresh adventure. Mom was always reluctant to allow me out of her sight, but Dad persuaded me to be independent and to enjoy the company of my sighted friends. I often heard Dad telling Mom, "Let him go. He'll be okay." Mom would reply, "If he kills himself it'll be your fault."

My fear of death was hardly paramount. All that concerned me was to do the things the other kids did, or at least to be with other kids when they did things I couldn't do, like playing volleyball.

If the Turnbull twins were not available, Peggy could usually be persuaded to take me out. Peggy taught me how to swim. She was probably sorry that she had done so because once I was in the sea I refused to get out. One day after I had made her stand around in the surf for a couple of hours, she got her own back by taking me into deep water and yelling "Shark!" Residual memories of Mr. Oooh bubbled to the surface of my mind. In utter terror I thrashed about in circles until Peggy mercifully guided me to the beach.

Looking back on those years, I recognize Peggy's incredible patience with me. She had her own friends and her own pastimes, but I always had priority on her calendar. I never fully appreciated her selflessness, even when she saved her pocket money and took me to an amusement park in spite of my being forbidden to go there by our mother.

The Turnbull twins and the other friends my own age often flattered me by forgetting I was blind. I would be playing with them on the beach or in a park and suddenly find myself alone, my companions forgetting that I couldn't find my way home on my own. When I had not returned home for dinner, Mom would phone the mother of the twins to find out where I was. I would be discovered immobile in the place where they had left me.

Frankie Bakey, two years older than the twins and I, took advantage of my blindness when he introduced us to the skills and thrills of shoplifting. Our plans laid as carefully as a military campaign, the four of us entered a candy store. I deliberately crashed into the store's owner and scattered my marbles on the floor. While the sympathetic proprietor helped me retrieve my property, the other kids helped themselves to candy. Safely outside, we shared the spoils. My pride in playing a critical role in these forays far outweighed any immediate burden of conscience. Perhaps what stopped me as a six- or seven-year-old from entering into a career of crime was the echo of my grandmother's warning about the fire and brimstone that awaited thieves—as well as boys who didn't eat their spinach.

There may have been another reason why pinching candy lost its appeal. My elder sister, Jean, was working for Mayor Hynes in Boston. I saw little of her but when she arrived for a rare weekend at home she always brought me more chocolate and chewing gum than I could consume. I still associate Jean with the smell of spearmint. Apart from providing me with a store of candy, her role in my early life was very small.

At Scituate, Dad was responsible for another development that made me not merely a member of the gang but monarch of the block. Even Frankie Bakey had to give way to my new prestige.

I was in the house washing my hands for supper when I heard Dad's imperious command. "Out here, Tommy. Something to show you." The slight slur of his tongue moved his accent closer to pure Limerick—a signal that he had been quenching his summer thirst. Dad and a friend had bought a pony. The animal was still in the trailer when I got out to the yard. At first I felt the hay on the floor and then hoofs and quarters. The pony's name was Brownie, but I called him Tucky because when I first touched him his blanket felt like a shirt that had slipped from a pair of pants and needed tucking in.

Dad dumped me on Tucky's back and led me around the block. Blind Tommy was instantly the most envied kid in town; and among my peers it became crucial to earn my favor for a ride.

But one evening, without my sanction, Dad borrowed Tucky to go to the local banquet of the Scituate Beach Association. Much later I pieced the story together. It seems that the mayor was there and the ladies who ran the annual flower show. Suddenly conversation died and the music stopped. Whooping like a cowpuncher, Porky Sullivan rode into the ballroom on Tucky. Reaching the center of the room, Dad tried to stand in the stirrups. The saddle began to slip—it was like a scene from a Marx Brothers movie, as it was described to me later—and Dad slid slowly under Tucky's belly. Before my father was energetically removed from the dignified assembly, the pony left a pile of manure directly under the chandelier.

Dad did not return by the shortest route. It took a case and a half of beer to quench his daily thirst, and predominantly Irish Scituate was not short of bars. Eventually reaching home and dismounting, he forgot to close the garden gate on Tucky. He was undressing in front of the bedroom window when he saw the pony leave the corral and trot down the road. Dressed only in his shorts, Dad chased the animal up the street, breathlessly catching up to him in the garden of one of the flower-show ladies.

Poor Tucky had had enough of Dad's curses. The pony kicked out and sprawled Dad across the petunias. The night was balmy and there are worse couches than a flower bed. When Dad woke up at sunrise, Tucky had consumed the petunias and was literally making hay of some costly hybrid begonias. It took Dad some moments to appreciate that the legs that stood astride him belonged to a uniformed officer of the local police. The flower-show lady wasn't smiling either.

The town office ordered the banishment of Tucky under a local bylaw prohibiting the keeping of horses within the limits of the town.

Dad wasn't beaten, however, and, quick to defend his castle and kin, he phoned a friend, the city editor of the *Boston Globe*. A reporter and a photographer soon arrived. The next day the paper carried what the newsroom described as a "five-Kleenex story" about the poor little blind boy about to be deprived of his beloved pony by the heartless city fathers of Scituate. The story spawned the biggest local political issue of the summer, and it is still claimed that several Young Turk politicians got their start by championing the cause of Tucky and Tom Sullivan. That may be, but most importantly for me at the time, Tucky was allowed to stay—until the following year, when my mother, weary of cleaning out the makeshift stable, banished the pony to a home for crippled children.

While worshiping Dad, I resented Mom—unfairly. She had her obvious shortcomings, particularly in being overprotective of a boy who, though gravely handicapped, yearned most of all to live the kind of life that other kids lived. It was so easy for Dad to play the hero. He had virtually no responsibility for the day-to-day and hour-to-hour problems and challenges of my upbringing. It was so difficult for Mom to win my full affection because she was always nagging me. But then she always saw me bleeding and battered from collisions and completely incapable of doing many ordinary things that are learned naturally by sighted children.

My resentment mounted against Mom's disciplines

and guardianship, and yet in hindsight I appreciate what care she gave me. There was no one to show her how to cope with my training. Yet she instinctively understood the importance of teaching me how to dress myself and how to feed myself without spilling food or knocking over cups.

She showed me, for instance, that I could avoid putting on a shirt inside out by feeling for the manufacturer's tag inside the collar. She devised a way for me to eat by using a piece of bread in my left hand as a pusher to the fork.

When I was quite young she helped me avoid the habits that make so many blind people awkward, embarrassing and unattractive. She snapped at me whenever she found me picking at my eyes—a common practice among those born blind. Another habit of blind people is to turn the ear instead of the full face to a person who is talking to them. By the age of six, thanks to Mom's constant reprimands, I automatically pointed my nose in the direction of a voice. This listening like a sighted person may be one reason why many people, on meeting me for the first time, are unaware that I am blind.

Until Mom corrected and taught me, I had no idea how ugly the mouth could be if it was allowed to gape, or of the importance of a smile.

But Mom instructed me in so much more than courtesies and table manners. She introduced me, for instance, to flowers, giving me names for perfumes and for touch.

The first flower I knew by name was the geranium, which grows prolifically at Scituate. I was puzzled, I remember, because its leaves had the touch of velvet, yet its smell was acrid, ugly. It seemed to me that something that felt so attractive to my fingertips should have a pleasant smell.

My love of flowers, shrubs, trees was first generated

in quiet summer evenings in Scituate when Mom took me to a neighbor's garden. Color, of course, meant nothing to me, and means nothing still. Speak of red or green or yellow to a person who has never seen and imagination screeches to a halt. But flowers that smell, flowers silk-soft as a rose's petal, these enter the joy of those who have no sight.

Mom was careful too in making sure, both at West Roxbury and at Scituate, that room furniture was not changed about; if a new chair was placed in a familiar room she would warn me of its position. She trained Peggy and visiting friends to close doors. A half-open door is one of the major hazards for blind people. If I were to make a list of my thousand collisions, half-open doors would come ahead of every other obstacle.

Mom made it known to friends and relatives that she was to be pitied. I was the cross she had to bear. For some reason that would eventually be explained to her in heaven, she had been afflicted with a blind child. She believed that her Christian duty was to protect me from the harsh realities of the world.

"If only he had been a girl," I once heard her complaining to a neighbor. "But he's a wild one like his father. That's what frightens me."

The thought that I was like Dad exhilarated me. I would grow up and have hairy arms and know every swear word in the dictionary and many that weren't. I'd have friends like Specksy O'Keith and Jonesy Smith and bubble the water over my face when I shaved. I might even grow as tall as Dad, and he was surely as tall as a tree.

I am constantly surprised by how little people remember of their early youth. I believe a blind person's memories probe further into childhood and are more deeply etched because he is not confused by a multitude of visual images. A score of years now separate me from Tom McDonagh's company, but I

would instantly recognize him from the smell of his to-
bacco if he were to pass me in the street. I could list
the Red Sox team of 1951. If now I were to sit at the
table that once stretched the length of our porch in Scituate, I would immediately know it by its grain.

Memories of those summer holidays in the early '50s
meld together and yield only excitement and wonder,
laughter, health and rich friendship. How fortunate
that clairvoyance was not one of my gifts and that I
could not see the heartbreak just ahead.

4. Shamrock Surgery and a Second World

I should have been warned by the signs and omens. I woke up one morning in early autumn with a boil on my bottom. Then at breakfast Mom announced that she wanted Peggy and me out of the house as she was expecting an important visitor, darkly hinting the visitor was concerned with my future. As Peggy led me reluctantly to the front door, Mom urged final cautions.

"Keep your eye on him, Peggy, and don't let him fall in the mud." (I was always falling in mud.)

Our third halcyon summer at Scituate was over. I was six years old and we were back at West Roxbury. The first leaves of the fall were buzzing and scratching about the pavement. Peggy, sulking, tugged at my hand. I wanted to walk north, she south. My relationship with Peggy oscillated between fierce enmity and warm comradeship. I acknowledged that I could not get along too well without her. But her misfortune—and mine—was that she was a girl. Girls did not like climbing trees or building a fort or playing Robin Hood, with broomsticks for swords and garbage-can lids for shields.

However, in these early years, it was Peggy more than anyone else who forced me to live a near normal life. She was the one I played with most, and she insisted I play well because she became bored if I didn't.

How tiresome a walk can be, especially when you have a boil on your backside. Our tension and tempers mounted. Fratricidal war was declared. Peggy chose her battleground—a tunnel under a railroad overpass. She had deceitfully told me the trains traveled through the tunnel and not over it. In the middle of the tunnel she suddenly let go of my hand and shouted, "Train's coming!"

In fact there was. I could distinctly hear the distant rumble growing louder by the second. Here I was in total darkness standing directly in the path of the approaching juggernaut—or so I thought. Peggy's mocking laughter was soon drowned by the thunder and earthquake of the train reaching the overpass. I flung myself to the ground, praying that the steel wheels would not guillotine my head. While the train passed safely overhead, separated from me by several yards of reinforced concrete, I lay flattened in terror.

Peggy's sadistic deception now seems extreme; but Peggy all too often had sole charge of me, and I bedeviled her, I'm sure, with my energy and restless demands. At six that morning I had jumped on her tummy to wake her up, and when Peggy smoked behind the delicatessen or kissed the big O'Keefe boy who was always around I never lost the opportunity of tattling on her.

In retrospect I must admit that in the running battles we fought without quarter asked or given, we usually settled for a truce and, as is the way with children, accorded each other grudging respect which matured to warm affection.

But this day another incident occurred, the results of which might have been more serious than a heart palpitating with terror. We continued our walk and were crossing a parking lot. Once again Peggy let go of my hand, this time without thinking. Suddenly I was knocked to the asphalt by the bumper of a reversing car. Nothing was broken, but a wheel must have hit me because my ankle immediately ballooned up. Seeing that I was only slightly injured, Peggy switched her concern to the prospect of parental punishment for her failure to protect me from hazards.

Hoisting me to her shouder, she begged, "Tommy, promise to tell Mom you ran into the car and that it wasn't the car that ran into you."

I was still trying to work out Peggy's logic when we arrived back home, there to meet a lady named Miss Kelly, the important visitor for whom Mom had vacuumed carpets and polished furniture.

Miss Kelly was a social worker of the kind that likes to tap the heads of small boys and coo in editorial "we"s.

"Well, Tommy, we are going to have a little game," she said. "We are going to find out just how clever we are."

I was in no mood for games. The boil on my buttocks throbbed when Miss Kelly made me sit at the dining-room table, and I knew my painfully aching ankle, now Ace-bandaged, would restrict for a while the only games I really enjoyed—ball games and hide-and-go-seek played with my street gang. It was obvious to me that I ought to get through Miss Kelly's table games as fast as possible. I had not heard of IQ tests, of Messrs Binet and Wechsler, who invented them, or of Mr. Hayes, who had adapted the standard IQ tests for blind children.

The first test was to make a square with about a dozen blocks of wood of different shapes. Then Miss Kelly rattled off numbers in growing sequence and asked me to repeat them, first in the recited order and then backward. Suspecting that if I made a mistake she would prolong these absurd diversions, I concentrated hard and gave both questions and answers the focus of my total attention.

Half an hour later I heard Miss Kelly speaking to my mother in the kind of awed whisper used in church. "Did you know, Mrs. Sullivan, that you have a genius in your family!"

Genius? It was the first time I had heard the word,

and I remember wondering whether it was some relation of the benevolent slave who appeared when Aladdin rubbed his lamp. In my innocence I did not know that I had been entered in the special advanced class of the kindergarten of the Perkins School for the Blind in Waterton, Massachusetts. Had I known, I would have maneuvered those wooden blocks into figures of eight and recited those digits like a village idiot.

But my day of disaster was not yet over. Dad returned home, trumpeting with Irish pride. "Sure 'n' the little son of a bitch's a genius. He's my son!"

Dad had the answer to everything, including an infallible treatment for boils. "An old Irish remedy," he told me as he pulled down my pants and bent me over a pillow. The remedy was indeed as simple as he pronounced. He filled a whiskey bottle with boiling water, sealing off the neck with a square of gauze. With initial gentleness he turned the bottle upside down and covered the inflamed and throbbing area with the gauze pad. Then with a triumphant "Here we go!" he pulled the gauze away so that the scalding water was in direct contact with the angry pustule on my bottom.

I've heard of acrobatics of tomcats on being deprived of their gender, and if I had not been facing the door instead of the bedroom window, I think I would have been self-propelled out onto the manicured lawn of the O'Keefes on the other side of Greaton Road.

But the memory of agony is, thank God, easily expunged. I can swear, however, that that ancient Irish remedy for boils works miraculously. I recommend it for anyone who has the fortitude to survive the pain.

Shortly after this shamrock surgery, my parents took me the twenty miles to the Perkins School. It was a rather silent journey. Answers to my questions were mostly given in muted, staccato sentences. Yes, I was going to have to stay at Perkins through the week, but I could come home every weekend. Yes, I was going to learn important things—like how to read in Braille. Yes, there would be other children there, all blind like me, and there would be special games and special teachers who understood the problems of blind children. My mind churned with this data. Who wants to learn to read when you can learn from the radio or hear from Mom or Peggy the most exciting stories in the world? When you are a blood-sealed member of the Scituate and Greaton Road gangs, who wants to play with blind kids? Who wants special teachers when you have sisters and a father and mother and an Uncle Joe—people who love you and who teach you everything you need to know?

"Here we are," said Mom. "We are turning in at the gates. Exciting, isn't it?"

Exciting? Somewhere in my small bowels a lump of ice was forming. The car stopped. We got out and went through a door toward an unctuous voice saying, "Mr. and Mrs. Sullivan? Ah, yes, so this is little Tommy. Come along now; we'll go and meet the other children."

And so I entered bedlam. Gettysburg after the armies had disengaged could not have sounded more tragic. Small children were crying as if mortally wounded. A score of blind children were being torn for the first time from the security of their homes and their parents. Above the childish wails I could hear the sobs of women and even the rare noise of men weeping.

My one passionate, overwhelming, instinctive thought was to break loose, to get out, to flee this cacophony of tragedy. But where to run? Darkness and bodies surrounded me. I resorted to my nursery strategy. I lay on the floor and kicked and clawed and screamed. I was ready to bruise and gouge the face of anyone within reach. Dad eventually pinioned my arms and lifted me up.

"Tommy, be brave now. Sure 'n' you're a Sullivan.

You're not an Italian kid; you're not a Jew, not a nigger. You're Irish. You gotta learn things, Tommy." Dad talked as if his fist was in his mouth. I had never heard him speak like this before. Mom blew her nose again and again.

Then my parents were gone. I shouted their names, but no one came to me. The other parents were too busy comforting their own children. The wailing continued all about me. I found a wall and in a state of panic felt my way along it until I reached an open door, a short passage and another door. Fresh air gave me renewed hope of finding the security of my parents' hands. They had to be out here somewhere. It was inconceivable that they could actually leave me in this terrible place.

Shouting "Mom!" "Dad!" and with my arms moving like a swimmer's breast stroke, I wandered aimlessly across some grass. Now I was lost and experiencing the raw emotion of emptiness. The grass led me nowhere. Utterly desolate, I lay face down and wept. If I were to choose the loneliest moment in my life, I think I would pick this one. In later years I was to experience times of spiritual agony, of acute physical pain and true peril. But this moment was drained of hope by what seemed to me to be the dark treachery of those I loved most.

Then I heard footsteps and a melodious voice asking, "You're one of the new children, aren't you? I'll show you where to go."

She was a stranger, but I instantly buried my face in the warmth of her breast. Then she began to sing very quietly, beautifully.

Not many years later that same voice, the voice of Joan Baez, who spent a year or two on the staff at Perkins, became internationally famous.

I suppose Miss Baez led me back to the dorm, and I suppose I ate something that evening before I went to bed, but the next thing I remember is being in a bedroom which I found myself sharing with another six-year-old, Billy Nicholson. In his own anguish, Billy was rocking back and forth on the straw mattress, causing the springs to squeak. Every now and again he emitted shuddering sobs and cries of "I want Mommy." I wanted my mother too. I wanted her to tuck me in, to read a story and to kiss me good night in a manner familiar since the mists of infancy. Yet as I began to feel sorry for Billy, who was obviously even more distressed than I was, my self-pity began to ebb.

"Hey, Billy," I said without enthusiasm. "Bet you can't do a somersault."

Billy's sobs grew louder.

"Watch me," I said (a figure of speech, of course, but I knew he could hear me, and at this stage of my life what was the difference?) and I rolled over the straw mattress. The bedsprings squeaked attractively.

Billy wailed.

I felt my way to his bed. "It's easy," I explained. "Put your hand on my feet," and I executed a somersault that even Peggy might have applauded.

Between sobs Billy said, "I can do that."

"Betcha can't," I challenged.

Within a few minutes, a dry-eyed Billy was rivaling my own acrobatics. I was just demonstrating a head-stand when the housemother opened the door. The sound of a woman's voice sent Billy into a fresh paroxysm of sobs. The housemother sat on his bed and hugged Billy to her enormous bosom, soothingly telling him, "You'll be all right, dear, you'll be all right."

"Billy's all right," I countered and then, unkindly, "He was okay until you came."

But Miss Harrison, a kindly soul by nature, had been told that the answer for first-night tears at school was coddling, not somersaults. Billy eventually cried himself to sleep while I continued perfecting somersaults.

We were awakened by a loud electric bell. I naturally began shouting, "Fire! Fire!" The house-mother looked in to assure two panicking small boys that this was the "get-up" bell—the first of countless bells that would govern the comings and goings of my school life over he next twelve years.

Breakfast was a chaos of spilled cereal and broken mugs, colliding bodies and whimpers. There followed instructions that all children had to be registered. We were told to grasp the shirt or dress of the child in front of us. Soon twenty blind children were snaking down corridors toward the mysterious rite of registration. The boy whose shirt I had gripped turned about and introduced himself as Ernie.

"Wanna bite?" asked Ernie Anderson as he shoved a half-eaten apple into my mouth. If Newton tied up the laws of gravity with an apple, Ernie cemented the bonds of friendship with half a Canadian pippin. It was a friendship that would last down through the long years and support us through pints of tears and gallons of laughter, through challenges, defeats and conquests. We became a rebellious trio when Jerry Pierce joined us. I first met Jerry in the small advanced class of the kindgergarten, along with two girls, Phyllis Mitchell and Bonnie Masters.

Girls were, of course, only girls, fragile, simpering creatures who would never dare to walk a wall and who tattled every time you twisted their arm or pulled their hair. I should exempt Sandy McPherson from the generalization. Sandy would hit back when I hit her. I got on well with Sandy. It was to be a good many years before I found out that, in Max Beerbohm's phrase, "Girls are a sex on their own, so to speak," and possessed attributes—well—of extraordinary fascination.

My first week at school is now a sort of photo album in my mind, with pictures ranging from sublime through ridiculous to revolting. Sublime moments included the discovery of a merry-go-round in the playground, the feel of modeling clay, the near escape, at least for an hour, of Ernie, Jerry and myself when we explored the forbidden field known as Brooks Hill behind one of the buildings. The ridiculous included the reading by our class teacher of "Jack and the Beanstalk." I, who had already ventured via radio with Tom Sawyer and Huck Finn, was insultingly urged to tremble before fairy story giants! Among the disgusting moments was having to sit at table with kids who ate like animals. I seemed to be the only child whose mother had taught him how to wield a spoon and fork. Worse still was the school toilet, always puddled. To this day, when I'm in a public toilet I find myself automatically lifting my feet to avoid the imagined "oosh" surrounding the stalls.

My world was now split into two parts, each one orbiting in the darkness of space as independently from the other, seemingly, as Mars and Venus. One world was surrounded by the high fence of the Perkins School for the Blind, which, let me say before we explore further, may well be the best blind school anywhere. The other world consisted of Greaton Road, West Roxbury, and the salted, sun-splashed town of Scituate. My spaceship between these worlds was a 1952 Oldsmobile, shuttling back and forth weekends or vacations. The spaceship's first pilot was my father, with a back-up crew comprising my mother and later Peggy.

In both worlds I had my friends and enemies, my joys and phobias. There was no other contact between the worlds, no blending of experiences. There was no question which world I preferred, but I would have been hard pressed to decide priorities and loyalties if compelled to choose between my classmates and my sighted street gangs, between Ernie and Jerry in the one world and the Turnbull twins, Paul Ward, and Billy and Mike Hannon in the other.

My first year at school, as in most kindergartens, was little more than a play year. It was not until I was seven and in grammar school that I started to learn anything worthwhile, including Braille.

To the sighted, Braille has always been a mystery, akin to crystal balls and card tricks. Actually, blind children learn Braille with no more difficulty than a sighted child has learning to read. Braille cards are substituted for a blackboard and, in short order, if the child has average intelligence his fingertips are reading A, B, C, then words, then sentences, paragraphs, pages and eventually books.

Perhaps the most exciting of my early instruction at Perkins was my introduction to the museum. There stuffed animals, including birds and fish, enabled me to find out, for instance, the dimensions of a bear—a sobering discovery which will surely trigger caution should I ever find myself alone in the forests of Yellowstone Park. From models of towns I learned to my amazement that the roofs of houses are not flat, and how roads intersect, and how tall are high-rise buildings compared with suburban homes.

The discovery of sizes and dimensions was what amazed me most. From pictures in their first books, sighted children quickly comprehend the length of a giraffe's neck, for instance, or the enormous size of an ocean liner. The giraffe or the liner is usually juxtaposed to a human figure. But for a child who has never seen his hands, it is almost impossible to imagine a living creature more than two stories tall or a ship as long as five football fields.

For a blind child, distance is related to time. It takes five minutes to walk to the delicatessen or an hour to drive from one town to another. As I grew up I never ceased to be amazed by dimensions—amazed, for in-

stance, that a golfer can hit a ball 250 yards or that
from the top of a mountain the eye can see fifty miles.
Fifty miles! What is this thing called vision that can at
the same time allow an eye to look at an extended in-
dex finger and a mountain peak or even the moon?

Ernie had a precise, mathematical mind. He found it
much easier than I to understand bigness and smallness
and that everything had length and depth and height.
He showed early evidence of becoming the first-class
physicist he is today. Jerry was uncoordinated, gutsy,
an adventurer. He was ready to try any new experience
without calculating the dangers. Maybe because I was
physically stronger, but essentially, I believe, because I
had played with sighted friends, I was the initiator, the
leader of the trio. Whether or not I knew the answer to
the teacher's question, I was always the first to raise
my hand in class. I started to introduce the Sullivan-
rules games and I was naturally the team captain.

It was easy to be the best of the blind. But being the
best at Perkins gave me a false sense of superiority. At
Perkins, for instance, we played a modified game of
football. I was the star player. But with the gang in
West Roxbury the kids would not let me run with the
ball. Among my sighted friends the game revolved
around me. Overcome by frustration and shame, I
knew I was the worst player on the field.

At an early age I began to understand why so many
blind children seek out the company of the blind and
shun the sighted world with its formidable challenges.

At the time I did not philosophize on the dichotomy
of my two worlds. I grew up as every child grows up,
accepting the loneliness and frustrations, the joys and
adventures as they evolved.

A typical adventure resulted from my discovery in
the Perkins museum of a suit of medieval armor. If it
was authentic, it must have been worn by a very small
knight indeed.

There was one boy in our class who, Ernie, Jerry and I soon discovered, was a little simple-minded and would do almost anything we told him. We persuaded the boy—let's call him Jim—to get inside the armor. In ten minutes it would be time for morning service in the school chapel nearby. We talked Jim into making his chapel entrance after the service had begun.

As chapel was part of the Perkins routine, it was for me scarcely surrounded by an odor of sanctity. This was the echoing chamber where the school principal made announcements, where we sang a hymn or two and prayed interdenominationally for our well-being. About midway through the short service, a member of the staff read from the Bible and that day for some reason he favored the ponderous Book of Deuteronomy. From the lectern, then, on the day when we had strapped Jim into the suit of armor, the staff member was boldly calling our attention to Deuteronomy, Chapter 24.

" 'When a man hath taken a wife and married her,' " intoned the voice from the lectern, " 'and it come to pass that she find no favor in his eyes because he hath found some uncleanness in her, then let him write a bill of divorcement ... And when she is departed out of his house ...' "

It was at this point that Jim made his dramatic entrance, signaled initially by the noise made by a garbage can being dragged to the front sidewalk. Then, as Jim turned into the paved aisle, the noise sounded like Providential vengeance against those who broke the Pentateuchal law.

The ultimate crescendo came when Jim, now about halfway down the aisle, tripped and fell. The words of Deuteronomy were silenced and I never did check up on what happens to unclean ladies who leave their homes carrying bills of divorcement!

Principals of schools have their ways of finding out

who cause campus uproars. The rebellious trio, Jerry, Ernie and I, were ordered to report to the principal's office, and for punishment were sent home for two weeks. This was the first of eleven occasions (a yet unsurpassed record) on which I was sent home from Perkins. I don't recall ever shedding a remorseful tear on any member of my family who came to get me.

When Dad picked me up that first time, he scolded me in a voice that threatened to shatter the chapel's stained-glass windows, profoundly impressing the Perkins principal. But once outside the Perkins gates, Dad roared with laughter at my escapade.

5. House Divided, a Hero Flawed

Dad was everything a child could ask for in his father. He smelled like a man—of cigars, beer, sweat and tweed coats. He talked in gravelly Irish, using the limited but highly colorful vocabulary of the Roxbury streets and bars. He walked purposefully, with stolid, metered steps. I had the impression that his fists were perpetually clenched and held in front of him, ever ready for an argument or a donnybrook. Had Dad been born a century or two earlier, he might have captained a pirate ship or, with spurs and gun, helped to open up the West. Dad naturally attracted to him men ready to drink life to the last drop in the cup—for that matter, to the last drop in the bottle.

In the '30s Dad had been a bootlegger. He worked for a prominent Boston family running small booze boats from the big ships. He had a spell as a prize fighter and displayed a dozen trophies on a shelf behind his bar. He made two fortunes and lost them both. I keep expecting him to make a third.

In the '60s Dad lost a five-year tax battle with the government and was ordered to pay $700,000 in back taxes. It was completely in character when he collected the whole sum in one-dollar bills and dumped the cartons on the steps of Boston's City Hall. He stepped back, arms akimbo, and told the revenue clerks, in language that singed the lawn, to get on their knees and pick up the spoils.

A year before this tax case was settled, Dad had bought a twenty-two-room mansion in Milton, Massachusetts, and staffed it with maids, cook and gardeners. After the tax settlement, his fortune was seized. We returned to a modest home and even occasionally to real hunger.

In his relationship with me, Dad was determined that I should, despite my handicap, become as aggressively male as he. There was to be no cushioning or cosseting of little Tom. While my mother endeavored to keep me at home as much as possible, Dad encouraged me to go out into the street and make friends. It was through Dad's games that I got to know Paul Ward, Billy and Mike Hannon and other boys who formed the nucleus of the Greaton Road gang. The tougher my friends, the more he liked them. He helped us build a gang headquarters in empty offices above his bar and he equipped one room with a boxing ring, urging Paul, Billy and Mike to teach me how to fight.

A typical incident illustrates Dad's attitude to me. One evening when I was about eight years old, the gang was creating mayhem in Greaton Road. We were thumping fences, ringing doorbells and kicking cans down the sidewalk. Suddenly a powerful woman, a new neighbor, burst through a front door and grabbed the first boy in sight. The other kids had fled, each thinking that I was holding the elbow of another. The infuriated woman began to beat me over the back and shoulders with a broomstick. My cries of pain and protest brought Dad up the street. Seeing what was happening to his son and knowing it was punishment deserved, he urged the woman to beat me the harder. Recognizing Dad, and knowing that he had a blind son, the woman was suddenly overcome with confusion and alarm.

"Beat the livin' daylights out of the little bastard," yelled Dad over her apologies.

Yet on other occasions my father could be gentler than a nun. He devised a basket with a buzzer so that I became almost as accurate at shooting a ball as my sighted peers—indeed, more accurate at twilight. Dad in fact proposed that I even up the odds by taking people on when the light had faded. What marbles or candy or cash I had lost in the daylight I recouped at nightfall!

Dad was a showman, a man of boundless spirit and enthusiasm. Every Christmas Eve of my first nine years he climbed the roof, where he played the role of Santa Claus, shouting "Ho! Ho! Ho!" down the chimney and jingling bells with ever more vigor. I was the last kid in the neighborhood to discover the truth about Santa Claus.

Certainly it was Santa Claus who brought me a tandem bicycle on my ninth Christmas, and it was Dad and Uncle Joe who all but destroyed the machine when they test-ran it down Greaton Road. I heard the crash and horrendous oaths from fifty yards away. When I learned that the handlebars had been smashed, I petulantly insisted that Dad get the bike repaired immediately. As all the repair stores were closed for the holiday, Dad had to take the bike twenty miles to a friend who owned a back-yard welding apparatus. He spent six hours that Christmas fixing up my bike.

But if Dad occasionally demonstrated saintlike attributes, more often he seemed possessed by a devil—perhaps even a legion of devils.

We were in Scituate the following summer when I discovered that my hero was flawed. I was well aware that he drank heavily, aware that many of his friends of both sexes were listed on the police files, aware that his normal vocabulary included words not then found in Webster's—words that, when I repeated them in our living room, earned me a soapy mouthwash from my mother. But the real flaw in my father's character was as unexpected to me as it was tragic for him and our family.

Any anniversary was good enough reason for Dad to celebrate, but Labor Day was an excuse to order liquor enough to float a fleet. Emboldened by liquor he had consumed through a thirsty afternoon at his own bar, the Dublin Tavern, Dad arrived at the Scituate house on a Sunday afternoon with a woman who, my mother soon saw, was more than just a friend. The first sign of trouble I picked up was when I heard Mom shouting at the woman to leave the house. Up to this point I had never known Mom to turn away any of Dad's friends. What started as a minor domestic squabble quickly shifted into uproar.

Suddenly the party, which was just getting into stride and had seemed destined to lead to a Monday dawn of belches, bacon and eggs, began to die. Guests were mumbling apologies and leaving; some left without apologies. Peggy and I were sent to bed. Jean, now living an independent life, was not at home.

At about midnight I was awakened by angry cries from my parents' bedroom. Then, as if watching a still-smoldering forest fire that suddenly flares up again, I was suddenly aware of new alarms and fresh danger.

Mom, by nature so even-tempered, the perfect foil to Dad's volatile, tempestuous character, had raised her voice in shrill protest.

"You're a bum," she was shouting. "Look what you're doing to our family!"

Dad shouted back, "Damn it, shut up, you bitch!"

A door was slammed, it opened and slammed again. The noise of accusation, abuse and countercharge was now outside my bedroom. Peggy was awakened. I heard her crying, pleading with Mom and Dad. I jumped from bed and reached the corridor just at the moment when Dad struck out at Mom, throwing her to the floor with a sickening thud. Somewhere, a yard or two beyond me, Dad stood grunting threats and oaths, his words slurring. I hurled myself toward him, butting my head into his stomach, flailing my fists at the giant.

"Stop it! Stop it!" I screamed, my fear and fury

driving me at him. He scooped me up, holding me to his chest. I clawed at his face while he bellowed at the whimpering woman and girl on the floor.

Dad's chest was heaving from exertion, his throat rasping like an animal's. When he wrenched my fingers from his face I thought he was going to hurl me at Mom. Instead he turned on his heel and, still holding me, lurched toward his bedroom. From the doorway he turned once more and thundered, "Tommy's the only one I love."

Love! Hate! My mind was a tempest of terror and confusion. I thought Mom might be dead.

I can still hear the sound of Mom hitting the floor. For me it was the sound of murder.

Dad threw me on his bed and got in beside me. I learned later that Mom slept with Peggy that night—if either of them slept at all. I didn't. Shivering, I listened to my father's drunken snores through the night until I heard the noise of traffic heralding another new day.

From that midnight, the world that had spun so surely on its axis slid out of kilter. My parents never again had any normal relationship. Dad often did not come home for four or five days, or was even away for a full week at a time. The revelry of the Irish weekend parties on the porch at Scituate ceased altogether. My gay and dashing father, who had taught me how to hit a ball, how to ride, who had entertained me by the hour with preposterous Irish tales and stories of prize fights, became a dour, sullen, secretive man, unreliable and completely unpredictable.

Although his innate kindness was reserved for me alone, he made and broke promises with what I could only think was cruel indifference. He would promise to take me to a ball game or a movie, but he would not turn up. Or if he did come home he would be so drunk that he would yell abuse at Mom or go straight to bed.

Both at Scituate and at West Roxbury I would often

lie awake listening for the sound of his car, one part of
my mind hoping he would return and be his old, rambunctious self again, the other part praying that he
would leave Mom, Peggy and me alone in peace.

One Saturday, after Dad had failed to take me to a
promised Red Sox game, he arrived home late and aggressively drunk. He at once found a scapegoat in
Mom, raking up an incident of years before I was born
when Mom, tired of too many lonely evenings, had
gone to a dance with a woman friend. The woman
friend, her partner and another man had offered to
drive Mom home. The car had been involved in an accident, which was reported in the local newspaper. Dad
had accused Mom then of infidelity. The incident was
grimly compounded when, two weeks later, the driver
of the car was found dead at the foot of a fire escape.
This long-festering abscess of suspicion had flared from
time to time over the decade. It flared once again this
night.

Uttering vile accusations and threatening to beat
Mom, Dad staggered upstairs to bed. From my own
bed I heard his snores and Mom's weeping. My
eleven-year-old mind churned with anger and with
hatred for him. Waiting until I was sure both Mom and
Peggy were asleep in the room they now shared, I
descended to the kitchen and found a six-inch
butcher's knife, its blade newly honed.

My heart thumping, my body shivering, my mouth
sticky with mucus, I reclimbed the stairs. Dad's bedroom door was ajar. I stood in the doorway for a few
moments, feeling faint from my intention—to end with
a thrust of the knife the revolting humiliation of my
mother. I remember wondering how I should kill him.
Should I stab his head or his heart? Would I waken
Dad if I fumbled for his chest? Would he scream or
gurgle—like the sounds of death in radio plays? The
dominant thought, though, was that never again would

Mom suffer the drunken abuse and brutality I had witnessed that evening.

Strangely enough, the consequences of what I was about to do did not occur to me—a juvenile court trial, perhaps permanent incarceration in a mental institution or in a home for delinquents. I saw myself only as a defender of the right, a champion of a frail woman I loved; I felt only desperation to rid myself of tension I couldn't understand.

Dad's snores guided me to his pillow. I put out my hand and touched bared muscled shoulders and his neck. With my other hand I brought the blade down until it rested on the oscillating Adam's apple. I am not sure how long I stood there in my pajamas by Dad's bed, he totally oblivious to the blade hovering over his jugular.

I wonder how many have testified to the intervention of a third force—call it fate, God, whatever—at the height of a crisis. At the beginning of this story I hinted at such intervention when my daughter was drowning in a pool. It was the same now. The cyclone in my mind stilled, and then an image rose up through the coils and convolutions of the gray matter in my skull: a memory of Dad patiently pitching his volleyball to my baseball bat. Again I heard his triumphant shout as I eventually made connection. I remembered how he threw me in the air, exhilarated by the small triumph of his sightless son.

The flash of memory was a catalyst to tears. For a moment or two longer I kept the blade across Dad's throat, he still unaware of his peril, I sobbing with emotion.

I loved him still. I loved the hero of my boyhood. I loved as a son loves a father who has poured out gifts uncounted and uncountable, not only the tangible gifts of toys and candy or a pony or a bicycle, but the greater gifts of his steady encouragement in my darkest moments, his unwavering faith in me, his loyalty, humor and rich comradeship—the gifts of simply being my father, the man who claimed he loved me more than he loved any other person on earth.

Many years later I told Dad how I had once held a blade across his throat and how, remembering his love, I had crept back downstairs and placed the knife, unbloodied, in the kitchen drawer. He scoffed at me, suggesting I had imagined the whole incident.

As I grew up, I came to understand somewhat better the mystery of Dad's dual personality; what made him both a monster and a martyr to his sense of honor. Later, as I researched the riddles of the human mind, I learned that we are all part saint, part sinner. Probe the depths of the finest souls and marsh gas will bubble to the surface, poisons which we label envy, lust, gluttony, temper—the seven mortal sins and more unnamed. How readily we see these sins in others; how reluctantly we smell them in ourselves.

But then I was still a boy, mystified and distressed by the clash between my parents. Yet being still a boy, I did not carry my distress like a ball and chain, or at least I cut loose the chain when I was with my Greaton Road gang, with Paul, Mike and Billy and the others, whose leader I now claimed to be.

Right of leadership was hard earned. It was an advantage, of course, to have more money in my pocket than my fellows (I was still grossly indulged by Dad and Uncle Joe), but the real tests came when I had to prove courage and prowess on the field. For instance, there was a free-standing wall ten or twelve feet high not far from home. During the winter the snow drifted and piled up against the wall.

"Betcha Tommy can't jump from the wall," dared Paul Ward.

The challenge taken up, the bet made—a dozen marbles or a double ice-cream cone—I was compelled to rashness. I was scared stiff, of course, for I had no idea how far I had to fall. What the gang was really doing was to use me, not for the first time, as a guinea pig. If I broke my neck or leg, the other members of the gang would not have to follow suit. Billy Hannon guided me along a precarious walk to the high point of the wall, and then he turned me sideways for the leap.

It is a misconception that because a blind person does not see danger, he does not fear it. I believe the opposite is true. A sighted person can weigh and measure the hazards. With the sightless person, imagination often goes berserk. I was expected to leap into space, a leap I knew must be formidable because no other member of my gang was ready to jump first. Yet not only Tommy Sullivan himself but sacred honor and the need for equality poised precariously together on the wall. To chicken out would have been to give up at once my hard-earned and coveted leadership. Concealing abject fear with what I hoped was a nonchalant grin, I leaped into dark oblivion. Years later I was to skydive from an aircraft, but when I think of falling through space, my memory instantly focuses on a twelve-foot jump into a snowdrift.

I survived, obviously, and how I enjoyed the sadistic pleasure of calling out, as if to execution, each member of the gang to make that heart-stopping leap. Looking back, I feel no pity for Billy, who wrenched his knee, or Mike, who cut his lip, or Paul, who somehow ripped his pants from cuff to crotch.

Though I was the leader of the squad, the other gang members achieved superior status when we contested for the Greaton Road boxing title. In boxing, I was the most popular opponent because, in effect, I was no more menacing than a punching bag. All I was able to do was whirl my arms in the direction of my opponent's footsteps. I may have learned the rudiments of the art and the Queensberry rules from Tussey Rus-

sell, but I was never able to protect my right ear or my
teeth from a straight left coming out of a tunnel of
darkness.

Back at Perkins, my handicap in sports largely disappeared. But I envied, even hated, those kids in my
class who had partial vision, for they could catch a
ball. If there was one thing above all others that caused
me frustration through unfulfilled yearning, it was my
inability to catch a ball.

Sport I loved beyond all else—sport in all its forms
and flex of muscle. Eventually I found some sports in
which I could excel, even gain a little glory. But in the
years between boyhood and adolescence I was ready
for any game, such as modified baseball, basketball and
track, that tested sinew but not sight.

My happiest hour at Perkins was not, however, on
the playground or when I was cooking up some prank
with Ernie and rebellious Jerry. The happiest hour was
three-thirty on Friday afternoon—the time when Mom
or, more rarely, Dad would pick me up for a weekend
at home. I was twelve when Dad came for me for the
last time. I was especially happy that he had come out
himself and told him at once that I hoped we could
spend the Saturday and Sunday together as a complete
family, recapturing the comradeship that had been ab-
sent so long.

His silence made me suspicious. "You're not coming
home," I blurted out, "because you're gonna see that
woman Mom is always talking about."

He swerved the car and braked it to a halt. For a
minute I wondered if he was going to hit me. Instead
he began to cry. Then words poured out of him like
soda from a bottle that's been shaken and uncorked.

Yes, there was another woman, and a baby too. He
had to look after them. He had to do his duty. Between
sobs the confession floundered on.

"You gotta understand, Tommy. Sure 'n' I love your

mother, but Sheila understands me. She don't nag me like your mom. . . . Don't blame me, Tommy. Now, you mustn't blame me. You gotta understand. . . ."

I told Dad I didn't want to hear any more. I put my hands over my ears. But I could still hear him talking about Sheila and Mom—how Sheila comforted him and cared for him, that she was "real brainy" and that she "cooked great." He went on about Mom rejecting his friends and not liking his late hours and not wanting to sleep with him anymore. His confession was often drowned out by a truck roaring past us on the highway. Once he tried to pull my hands away from my ears. He wanted me to hear everything. He admitted he drank too much and had done things to Mom he was sorry about. But Mom wouldn't forgive him. If Mom had forgiven him it would have been different. Sheila didn't mind his drinking. Sheila didn't reject his friends. Sheila liked him in bed with her . . . Sheila . . . Sheila . . . Sheila . . .

Then he spoke about me. He claimed he was the cause of my blindness. Mom had been upset with him when I was born. That was why I'd been born too early. He had made a mess of his life and of everyone else's too. Everything he touched "turned sour," he cried.

"Say something to me, Tommy. Say something, d'yer hear?"

I felt robbed, drained, sick in my stomach. Then I, a twelve-year-old boy from the Perkins School for the Blind, parked in a car by the highway, tried to counsel a grown man shrewd enough to make a fortune, a man with many influential friends. I told him that if he loved Mom and Peggy and Jean and me he should leave this other woman and come home. I told him that it would be okay, that things would be different.

I don't think Dad paid any attention to what I was

saying because he suddenly said, "Come and stay with me, Tommy. Come and live with me and Sheila."

I went to the house where Dad's mistress lived. I heard her speak. She was quite drunk. From a crib I heard a baby's cry. The child would carry the name of Sullivan, just like me, but it was illegitimate.

Over the next years the web of my father's personal life was to become ever more tangled—a web that not only enmeshed me in his conflicts but came close to stifling my own natural impulses to love any other human being.

He had forsaken a woman he had once loved very deeply for a woman who was a lush. Even a twelve-year-old boy could understand that.

Above the baby's cry I shouted, "I want to go home, Dad. Take me home to Mom."

6. Venus and Venalities

Two years after Dad's confession of sexual profligacy, I discovered sex for myself—on a dance floor. If this appears to be an overstatement, the excuse is that I mark the occasion as the first milestone of my varied sexual adventures, sad, sordid and sublime. I was fourteen and a freshman in the upper school at Perkins. As part of the institution's social-orientation program, sighted boys and girls were bussed in once a month for a dance. So it was that I found myself clasped to a girl called Sally, with whom I attempted to circle the floor to the music of Strauss.

Blind children are slow to mature sexually. The reason for this is that, unlike sighted adolescents, they cannot be visually aroused. The sighted pubescent boy's hormones are naturally stimulated by a glimpse of a girl's upper thigh on a swing or a classroom chair. He takes interest too when the eleven-year-old next door begins to fill out her sweater. The swish and sway of a short skirt and the jiggle of a small, rounded fanny transmit wake-up impulses to dormant male glands.

Denied these provocations and stimulations, the boys at Perkins remained sexually stagnant a year or eighteen months longer than the sighted boys at the neighborhood school. On my fourteenth birthday I knew as much about sex as a Pygmy knows about the law of relativity. However, Sally and the "Blue Danube" were responsible for shooting into my bloodstream a barrage of hormones. While my sex glands were still at the starting block, as it were, hers had beaten the gun. Sally possessed a splendid pneumatic chest, which rhythmically took up the Straussian cadences. As the school band thumped out the Viennese beat and as Sally's nylon-sheathed bosom pressed against my rib cage, I felt an extraordinary, exhilarating stirring in my loins.

The band played on. *Dum-dee-dee-dum-dee-dum-dum-dum.* My right hand increased pressure under Sally's shoulder blades and this in turn tightened the torque between us. As the "Blue Danube" moved to its climax, extraordinary things began to happen to my body. I was breathless when Sally led me to a bench against the wall.

I had no idea at the time (and none now) whether Sally's face matched the majesty of her bosom, whether she looked like Marilyn Monroe or a Mozambique monkey. Maybe somewhere out there in Boston or Baltimore, in St. Louis or in San Francisco, there is a Sally who will read this account of my adventures, a Sally who will recall that Strauss waltz and an eager fourteen-year-old whose face was flushed, whose mouth hung open and who answered her not a word as she made her charming exit from my life. I fear from early evidence that Sally may now be encased in heavy-duty corsetry. Yet for me she does not age. She stands frozen in time, a Medici Venus, at the crossroads of my puberty.

That night when I returned to my dormitory I was overwhelmed by mystery and a sense of profound alarm. My new roommate was Arnie, an eighteen-year-old who had only recently lost his sight. Though four years my senior, Arnie was partially in my care, for I had been appointed his guide around the school and through the new dark environment that for him was still frightening.

I told Arnie what had happened on the dance floor. He cleared his throat and said gravely, "You've probably made her pregnant."

"Pregnant?"

"She'll probably have your baby," said Arnie in a

New England twang. "You'll have to wait a month—maybe five weeks. You'll have to marry her, of course."

Terror now. A baby! Mine! Marry her! Was that how they were made? I mean as simply as that? Oh, God, what had I done!

"I don't even know her other name," I moaned. "Just Sally someone."

"Cool it," comforted Arnie. "Sometimes they don't have babies the first time." I grasped at this straw until Arnie added, "But they almost always do."

Saturday, two days later, I was home in West Roxbury and rushing to confession with Paul Ward and Billy and Mike Hannon. Although the gang were puzzled by my sense of urgency, I refused to tell them about my venal sin. When I had hinted at its magnitude, it was practical Paul who suggested that I confess to Father Flaherty—"because he's almost half deaf."

Through the screen I prepared Father Flaherty for the abomination to come.

"Bless me, Father. I confess to Almighty God and to you, Father, that I have sinned. These are my sins. I have been disobedient twelve times and I swore eight times." A pause, and then, "And, Father, I think I have made a girl pregnant. . . ."

If Sally wasn't pregnant, the silence was. Hopefully Father Flaherty had not heard me. Maybe he was asleep. (Billy had known him to sleep through a confession of stolen marbles.) But no such luck. My mumble had vibrated Father Flaherty's leathery eardrum. I heard his intake of breath before he asked, "How do you know this, my son?"

As previously to Arnie, so now to Father Flaherty I recounted my spontaneous physical response to Sally's proximity on the dance floor. Even as I recalled the pressure of her exquisite bosom I felt a fresh stirring in my loins. So the devil was still playing me havoc, even in this holy place. After I had stumbled through my story, I was amazed to hear a chuckle from behind the screen.

Before prescribing penance (ten Our Fathers and eight Hail Marys), Father Flaherty gave me a birds-and-bees lecture, assuring me in so many words that a combined barrier of wool and nylon would likely prove a 100-percent-effective form of birth control—a method, I subsequently conjectured, unlikely to have been debated in the Vatican.

"However," added Father Flaherty in a voice that dropped an octave, "you must always remember that the Church does not condone sexual union outside matrimony."

I was soon to discover a great deal more about sex than the blurred data that wheezed through the screen of Father Flaherty's confessional. A month later Dad sent a driver to pick me up at Perkins on a Friday afternoon. I was taken directly to one of Dad's six night-clubs, the one where he had his small and stuffy office. I hated the place. It smelled of stale cigar smoke and beer. But as soon as I entered the office this time, I picked up the smell of perfume.

"How old are you, boy?" asked Dad.

"Fourteen, sir."

"Time for you to learn about life," he said and then he introduced me to Betty and Helen. For a fee of $150 apiece, Dad had bought up Betty's and Helen's whole weekend, not for his own entertainment but for my instruction on, surely, the whole sexual ency-clopedia.

But a purchased tumble in an overperfumed boudoir and subsequent pawings behind pizza parlors or under the Scituate pier were neither the most important nor the most exciting features of my pubescent years.

Like an airliner beginning to move down the runway for takeoff, my whole life suddenly gathered momen-tum.

Sport now shifted from back-yard games with Sullivan rules into the high adventure of legitimate contest. Wrestling gave me the opportunity I'd been waiting for—a chance to test muscle, sinew, coordination and self-discipline not only against my Perkins classmates but, on a basis of equality, against those who had no physical handicap.

The man who helped me learn the art of wrestling, and along the way helped ease me out of the eddies of self-pity, was Dick Kamus, the Perkins wrestling coach.

Himself only partially sighted, Dick saw in the gangling kid before him not only a willingness to try hard but a potential to win. Had Dick not been my coach, my first wrestling match against a sighted opponent would surely have been my last.

My initial meeting with Dick was when he instructed the boys in my class to report to the gym. There he took each of us by the shoulders and threw us one by one to the floor. The other kids protested meekly, but I responded by getting off the floor and butting the coach in the stomach with my head.

"So you're the one with a temper," said Dick, laughing. "I'm going to teach you a contact sport where you may get hurt. But if you lose your temper you'll be no good."

Dick used two methods to teach us wrestling. First we went through the different movements and holds with him, feeling where his hands and feet were placed and the poise of his body. Then he gave a number to each of the movements. If he called three, for instance, we locked our hands around our opponent's knees. On the call of five we dropped our opponent and got on top of him.

At fourteen, I was the youngest member of the Perkins upper-school team. The hour before my first match I had to go to the bathroom twelve times. Then my name and weight were called. Rubber-legged, I walked to the mat, but instead of the anticipated roar of partisan encouragement, a surge of laughter swept through the gymnasium. I learned that I was the object of the mirth when Coach Kamus shouted at me as I got to the mat, "Your uniform's inside out."

In the locker room I had put on my tights and pants with the school colors (red and blue) against goose-pimpled flesh and left exposed to spectators the white fluff of the lining. I must have looked as if I'd dressed to play an Easter bunny. Across my backside flapped a label reading "Machine wash warm—tumble dry."

Shamed and shattered before my friends and rivals and, worse still, before my parents, who for my sake kept up a pretense of marriage and had come to see my first match, I turned to run back to the locker room. Then, during a momentary ebb of laughter, I heard Dick Kamus growl, "Quitting, Tom? I thought you were gutsy!" I hesitated, then turned once more toward the mat, thrusting out a trembling hand to a confident opponent. The match was over in thirty-seven seconds. I was thrashed!

My humiliation was followed by more pain. I wept alone in the shower, but Mom's tears and Dad's grim silence later hurt more than all the mocking laughter.

After each of my early matches Mom and Dad took me to a restaurant and invited me to choose anything on the menu. The meals were marked by awkward silences or by silly surface chatter which never fooled me. As a staunch Catholic, Mom refused to divorce Dad, who gave her an allowance to maintain the Greaton Road home. I still held on to a hope that as a family we could somehow return to the gaiety and happiness of my early years. Mom and Dad competed for my affection—Mom by keeping up the home with fussy care and Dad by giving me money whenever I asked for it and even when I didn't.

In my next five matches Mom and Dad heard five

referees pronounce my opponents outright winners. After one match Dad stormed the mat and acutely embarrassed me by protesting I'd been fouled. He was still bellowing obscenities when teachers ejected him from the gym.

Before my seventh match, even Dick Kamus told me I had no chance. "Your boy's three years older than you are, Tommy," he cautioned, "and he's never lost. But learn from him, eh?"

A curious effect of the coach's lack of confidence was my total freedom from pre-match nerves. No running to the bathroom this time. In fact, I was nonchalant as I shook hands with my opponent. No one in the gym was more surprised than I was when I took him down in the first period. In the second, he equaled the points with a reversal. In the third period I "escaped," and thus chalked up my first match win by a score of three to two.

Although I wasn't to lose again in 384 consecutive wrestling matches (a record that led me to a U.S. national title and an invitation to Olympic trials), this first win was the most exciting sports victory of my life. It dawned on me that I was no longer just a blind kid competing against other handicapped kids, a sightless boy for whom modified rules had to be devised. For the first time I had shown my family and friends, and all those people who had patted me on the head and pitied me, that I could hold my own in the sighted world. I had demonstrated that in a legitimate international sport that did not favor the handicapped, I, Tommy Sullivan, could win.

My blood boiled with exhilaration. Standing alone in the same shower where I had wept after my first match, I now stood, white-knuckled and grinding my teeth, deciding I wasn't going to be merely a wrestler, but a champion.

Now when Dick Kamus coached us, I stopped

fooling around with Ernie and Jerry and hung on to his
every word. I practiced the movements, the holds, the
rhythms, the reactions until I could have carried them
through in my sleep—and always that critical fraction
of a second faster than my opponents, real or imagined.

Wrestling was not without its pain and broken
bones. Since the match began with both wrestlers in
the standing position, I was almost always taken down
in the first period, when my sighted opponent had the
advantage. But because of my determination to win, I
always discovered inner reserves of strength. In one
match I was thrown to the second row of the bleachers
during the first period. I cracked two ribs, hit my head
and suffered a concussion. I still have no recollection
of the second and third periods of that match or of the
two other matches that afternoon in which I competed
and won.

As an adult wrestler I learned the art of "games-
manship" and how to take advantage of my blindness.
In one of my last matches, when I was being badly
mauled by a better wrestler, I deliberately pulled out
one of my plastic eyes (glaucoma had necessitated the
removal of my eyes when I was in Harvard). I yelled
to the referee for a time-out. My opponent took one
look at my face and threw up. The match was mine!

But at the age of fourteen, through wrestling I
wedged my foot in the door to the sighted world, the
world that almost everyone else took for granted. My
determination to barge my way through that door became brutal. Now I constantly searched about for ways
to enter the world of the nonhandicapped.

The next opportunity came about through music.

Male hormones had been fired into my arteries and
were working overtime. They reached the complex
cords of my throat. The treble that had been used to

summon the gang in Greaton Road had suddenly cracked into a tenor.

The upper-school chorus at Perkins is internationally known. Music is the most obvious cultural endeavor for the blind, although naturally not every unsighted person has any sense of pitch or the potential to be a musician. A continuing tragedy is that too many musically ungifted blind people persuade themselves that they should seek a career in music—a conviction that has led to much frustration and to hunger in back streets.

Neither scientist nor theologian has been able to explain why some people, sighted or unsighted, have this talent or that; why a Michelangelo, a Beethoven or a Shakespeare towers above his fellow mortals. But there is exciting new evidence from aptitudes research at the University of Southern California and elsewhere that almost everyone of normal intelligence can excel if he discovers the focus of his creative potential.

At Perkins there was much I resented, much I wanted to change and want to see changed today, yet because I had some talent and was given first-class coaching in music, I was led to an early discovery of my professional career.

At fifteen, every upper-school student was given a voice test. I was directed to a soundproof room where a maestro struck piano notes and invited me to match them. Five minutes later the maestro spun on his stool and said with high enthusiasm, "Tommy, you have a very fine voice indeed, and you have perfect pitch." If he had told me I'd just run the mile in three minutes or inherited the crown of Ruritania I could not have been more elated. Here, anyway, was another field in which I could compete with sighted people on a basis of equality. Music became my passion, eventually an art to take me to a life of independence and material comforts.

For this chance discovery of music I have to thank Dr. Paul Baugus. He was the musical director of the Perkins chorus, and although I was his Tommy the Menace, he had the forbearance to tolerate my outrageous conduct. He seemed to believe that he had found a "potential Caruso." Dr. Baugus was both a romantic and a Texan, thus prone to exaggeration. However, it was a period of my life when my ego was in need of every boost. The Baugus superlatives did me no serious damage!

In the Perkins chorus I teamed up with the only three black boys at the school. Paul, Earl and Ellis had sung spirituals in their home churches. One evening when they were singing outside their dormitory, I joined in and was at once invited to turn the trio into a quartet. Our extramural singing was pure fun, but when we tried to introduce our own "soul" descant into Handel's "Hallelujah" Chorus, Dr. Baugus had some sort of seizure that kept him off the podium for three days!

My piano teacher, Hank Santos, was a politically conscious black and a friend of Dr. Martin Luther King, Jr., to whom, a few years later, he introduced me. My first lessons in piano, particularly the interminable practicing of scales, wearied me. Sensitive to this boredom and my protestations, Mr. Santos was always willing to stop a lesson and talk about racial problems and the blacks' struggle for civil rights. Perhaps because I too am in a sense a member of a minority group and because I am unaffected by the color of a man's skin, Hank Santos's zeal and dreams captured my imagination. I found myself drawn into the equal-rights struggle, at least intellectually, and deeply attracted by the music and culture of the ghetto.

The blind learn music through Braille in the same way they learn to read and write. For piano music, the Braille notes are written on two lines—the right hand on the top line and the left hand on the lower line. The music is read and memorized measure by measure. A blind pianist reading Braille music can learn a whole concerto as quickly as a sighted player of equal competence can learn it from conventional musical notation. The blind student is usually slower in his early lessons, but his particularly sensitive hearing helps him to catch up and often to overtake the sighted player. (My ear was quicker than my fingers, and I used to cheat: Mr. Santos played a section and I was usually able to play it immediately without bothering to read the Braille music.)

For singing, I read the words with my left hand and the notes with my right, usually at the same time. Besides the piano, I learned to play recorder, harpsichord and drums, and before I left Perkins I had a well-rounded musical education. Mr. Santos had high hopes of my becoming a classical pianist. I loved playing in quartets, and particularly enjoyed Bach, but it was in singing that I began to excel.

For a Christmas concert in 1964, Arthur Fiedler invited the Perkins chorus to augment the Boston Conservatory chorus for a rendering of a difficult cantata by the Swiss composer Honegger. A well-known tenor scheduled to sing a solo in this work failed to turn up for the rehearsal at Symphony Hall. I had learned the part at school and was invited to stand in. Fiedler was apparently impressed, for after the rehearsal he invited me, through Dr. Baugus, to sing at the Boston Pops concert. I was nervous, but apparently sang the solo adequately because a few days later I was asked to sing the same part with the Washington Cathedral choir.

It was in the Washington Cathedral that the grandeur of music really got to me and I conceived the idea of making a musical career.

In the next semester I sang with the Perkins Glee Club for President Johnson at the White House. I

remember the sense of awe on being driven in the
school bus through the gates on Pennsylvania Avenue
and on being taken to the East Room. After this
concert, the President shook our hands and had a word
with each of us. He asked me how long I'd been blind
and what I planned to do with my life. I told him that
I wasn't sure of my career but that I wanted "to do
something important."

It must have been an unexpected answer because
Mr. Johnson paused several seconds, then said,
"There's something special for everyone to do.
Remember, no experience is a bad experience unless
you gain nothing from it."

This may not have been an original *bon mot,* but in
later years, when I reached nadirs of depression and
frustration and suffered my most serious setbacks, I always recalled Mr. Johnson's encouraging reflection.

When I was fifteen I began to receive instruction
crucial to a blind person. I remember a young teacher,
a woman of unlimited patience and determination who
had just graduated in peripatology—a science unfa-
miliar to those who have not visited a school for the
blind. This teacher, Cathy Riley, taught mobility with
the use of a cane. It was a seventh-grade course and as
important as any in the curriculum. There are two
peripatology cane techniques: for outdoors and in-
doors.

The indoor technique requires that the cane be held
with the arm extended across the body and moved
across the floor. Outdoors, the technique involves shifting the cane from side to side. As the left foot comes
forward, the cane swings to the right; and with the
right foot forward, the cane arcs to the left. But mobility instruction amounted to much more than how to
use a cane. The blind student is taught, for instance,
that when crossing a street to come up to a curb and
square his feet, thus making certain he is traveling

straight ahead. When Cathy first took me to a street crossing, I found it unnecessary to square my feet in the prescribed fashion. I simply crossed and continued down the sidewalk, avoiding a lamppost and a pedestrian and ducking under a low-slung tree branch.

Cathy was puzzled. "How did you know?"

"Know what?"

"That you were square to the curb and that the tree limb was there?"

"I just knew," I replied. "It's always like that."

"Can you see at all?" asked Cathy. "Perhaps shadows? Can you tell light from darkness?"

"No," I said. "I've never seen anything."

"Nothing?"

"Not the way you mean."

It was hard to explain and I thought about her question for a moment. Then I said, "I sort of see with my face."

We leaned against a wall at the street corner. I could hear people moving up and down the sidewalk and there we discussed "facial vision," the rare and priceless attribute that very few blind possess. I mentioned this earlier, likening facial vision to the natural radar of a bat or porpoise. Among the fifteen hundred totally blind students at Perkins while I was there, only two others to my knowledge possessed this rare sense. Facial vision was the reason why I moved faster, why I was more adventurous and more aggressive than my friends. Facial vision is not foolproof. If there were a slim object like a telegraph pole immediately ahead of me, I would most likely crash into it, as the vibrations have to be angled to register. For in spite of my facial vision, there were at least six occasions within a two-year period in the upper school when I knocked myself unconscious or was badly concussed from trying to walk through a concrete pillar or something like it. After one collision and concussion, I kept vomiting and

fainting for several days. Mom panicked and our
family doctor warned me "to take it easy and stop running around or your brain may be permanently damaged."

Stop running! He might as well have told me to cut
my throat.

Cathy Riley and I became close friends. Together
we conducted one of the first experiments on the electronic cane. I found it vastly inferior to facial radar.

The electronic cane functions like a metal detec-
tor—through increasing levels of sound. When the
cane is about twenty feet from an object, a low initial
warning is given. The pitch rises and the intensity of
the sound increases as the object is approached. The
cane has shortcomings. It does not, for instance, warn
of a curb or indicate how large an object is. The electronic cane serves a useful purpose for older people,
but for a young, athletic, blind person it is quite inadequate.

Increasingly sophisticated devices are being invented
for the blind. Among the latest inventions is the Opti-
con, a battery-operated machine that, when slid across
a page of print, raises the letters so they can be felt by
the fingertips. Scientists are now working on the
concept of being able to transform light and darkness
into physical sensations. It is possible that medical
scientists may eventually eliminate blindness altogether
by circumventing the opacity of a damaged eye. I don't
spend much time speculating on this possibility, or on
what I would like to see first—although I may do so
when science is much closer to the prospect.

In a way Cathy Riley taught me about love—not
sexual love, not love of a romp in a bedroom or the
sticky-handed pawing in the back seat of a car, but the
real love of a man for a woman. Cathy, one year married, spoke of her husband as if he were her alter ego, an
extension of her own personality. She told me quietly

of their anguish when their first baby was stillborn and how this domestic tragedy had deepened their marriage, their love for one another. I pondered her story as a new emotion. This was my first glimpse of married love as it is meant to be, married love as I would one day find it.

During my years at Perkins there had been many changes at home. Peggy had gone to college and Jean had got married. Dad continued to live with his mistress, whose second child was due shortly. Mom spent most of her time alone, and the loneliness she suffered was inexorably breaking down her spirit. Dad had prospered enormously from his six clubs. Whether on drunken impulse or as a salve to his conscience, he bought Mom a twenty-two-room house on twenty-one acres of ground in Milton, Massachusetts.

Our new neighbors did not speak in Boston Irish but in the accents of blue-blooded New England Yankees. The E. M. Loews, a well-known Jewish family, owners of a chain of theaters, also lived nearby. They kept a big stable of horses and during the summers I was there Mrs. Loew, a deeply compassionate woman, taught me to ride in a very English, schooled fashion.

It was this opportunity to ride on weekends and vacations in fair weather or foul that made our new big house even tolerable. When I thought of home I thought of Scituate in summer. My friends were there—the Turnbull twins, Paul Ward, Frankie Bakey and old Tom McDonagh, who continued to take me fishing. Shuffling through the happiest recollections of my mid-teen years, my mind constantly sweeps back to the comfortable silences alongside Tom McDonagh on a riverbank or in a boat, and to those sudden unexpected tugs that bent the pole and heralded the slap and flurry of a flounder at my feet.

I learned to water-ski in that year of our move to Milton. This was a sport that seemed to have been created especially for me. Yet I learned it, as I learned every new pastime, the hardest way. The first time I put on water skiis to slither across the smooth water of the North River, I finished up ignominiously, face down in a mudbank. But I was learning now to laugh at myself. And as no bones were broken, I pursued the sport until I mastered it.

That fall, back at Perkins, I received an urgent summons from the director's office. I assumed at once that someone had discovered I had smuggled beer into the dormitory. But the summons was more serious than that. The director told me that Mom had been hurt in a street accident. A driver was already waiting to take me to Milton Hospital.

Arriving at the hospital, I was taken to the intensive-care ward. I had had no idea that Mom was just a whisper away from death. Three hours earlier she had been crossing a rain-swept street, a sack of groceries in her arm. A driver jumping the red light had knocked her to the gutter; her spine was crushed, her right leg gravely fractured.

Dad was standing at the foot of the bed. He barely acknowledged my arrival. The attendant nurse led me to the pillow and left the room. I grasped Mom's hand, limp, unresponsive, and with my other hand felt the slings and pulleys of traction. I thought Mom was sleeping. In fact, she was in a coma. Suddenly Dad began talking as if I were not there, whispering as if he and Mom were quite alone.

"Ree, I love you. You know I love you. I've always loved you. You don't understand, Ree. You don't know. I'm sorry, Ree. I'm sorry."

I was puzzled, embarrassed, feeling as though I had been caught listening to a bedroom intimacy.

I called her name now. "Mom, it's me. I'm here. It's Tommy." I squeezed the limp hand and pressed it to my face. Perhaps some time elapsed—it's hard to remember. Then her fingers moved. I was to learn from Dad later that she opened her eyes for the first time since the car had struck her down.

Mom did not die, but in her four and a half months in the hospital and in the long months afterward in the big house, where she learned to walk again, her spirit died a little more. She bought long dresses to cover the misshapen leg, but her shattered confidence in life, in herself as an attractive woman, could not be veiled.

In painting portraits of my parents I am always tempted to portray Dad in bold, broad strokes. For my mother I use a finer brush, more muted tones. It is my father, though, who dominated my youth, over-shadowing the small-boned, simple Boston Irish woman he had married.

They once had loved each other; I'm sure of that. But I find it hard to understand how they had ever believed they could find lifetime partnership. I am told by many who have seen our family photo albums that Mom was an attractive woman. I know that she loved dancing, enjoyed playing hostess to my father's friends. The tragedy began, I think, when Mom responded with coldness and silence to the first signs of Dad's philandering. Perhaps only such a failure of feeling, her seeming indifference to my father's betrayal, can explain Dad's bizarre double life.

I forget whether it was Peggy or Jean who once laughingly reflected that the three of us were the products of the only three occasions that my parents slept together. This, of course, can hardly be true, but in searching for an explanation of my father's behavior, I think there may have been cause in Mom's failure to fight back, employing all the natural attributes of her femininity. If Mom had really competed, I think Dad's mistress, Sheila, would not have stood a chance.

But it is not my right nor my intention to analyze

my parents' marriage at any deeper level than where it affected me.

If, as is said, a home is a house with a heart inside it, I find it difficult to find the pulse in my own home unless I fumble back to my earliest memories. I remember too vividly Mom cringing before misfortune, and I recall the stream of "don'ts" she flung at her rebellious son. For me, Mom was always a fearful woman, fearful of all the real and imagined dangers she saw around her.

Yet as I peer behind the dominant figure of my father, I see a woman who gave me a quality of compassion and gentleness which surely helped me avoid taking the road of Porky Sullivan.

Although at the time I resented Mom's endless admonitions, I value them now. For instance, a blind person is especially prone to be egocentric and to talk constantly of himself. This is because so much of his external world is in his mind. Mom berated me whenever I was self-concerned and thus indirectly helped me find outside interests and fascination in the lives of other people.

I have often been asked if I wasn't bitter as a young child. I doubt whether in fact a young child is ever bitter; surely bitterness is an adult syndrome. I was confused, certainly, frustrated constantly, and often deeply hurt; but bitterness came later, spilling its acid over many memories of my childhood.

If there were some way we could change the patterns of our past, alter the course or corners of our travels, I would wish to have helped my mother understand the need to fight for Dad. Had Mom recognized the first signs of our endangered family life, perhaps she would have been able to heal the wounds before they festered.

Yet these are maturer thoughts. At the time of her accident I passionately hoped that tragedy would provide the opportunity for my parents to come together again. In my dreams I saw myself spending time with Dad on weekends, not in his stifling office but as master of his gracious home, a cheerful host to his friends, to my friends and to our neighbors.

However, after the accident, Dad went back to his mistress and the other children. Mom knew about "that other woman" but it was two or three years before she discovered that Dad had set up Sheila in a house of her own and that he was the father of Sheila's children. I felt I had to cover for Dad. I lied and made excuses for him only because of those words sobbed across a hospital bed to a crushed woman who had been born with a heart big enough to embrace and hold for a while even Porky Sullivan. I still continue to wonder what lives might have been changed if Mom had heard the words Dad uttered with so much honest and pathetic tenderness.

7. Perfume and Perfidy

For most people, memory is stirred through vision. Catching a brief glimpse of a stranger on an escalator may spark a sudden nostalgic flash. It may be the beaten gold of a sunset across a lake or the night reflections of a rain-swept city street that calls to mind a significant encounter. As he fingers souvenirs or laughs over home movies, the sighted person may recapture and relive an event of years ago.

My memory can be stirred by a question asked across a shop counter, by the fabric of a chair, the texture of a wooden bench, by the musty smell of a beach house or the acrid smell of burning leaves. In these ways people, a host of people, move out of the wings to walk across the stage of my mind.

The smell of a perfume, Chanel No. 5, brings alive for me a memory of a young woman physically so beautiful that she had modeled for *Playboy*'s centerfold, and so selfless by nature that she sacrificed a Hollywood prospect for the enormously demanding and underpaid work of teaching handicapped children.

I met Hope Francillon on the second day of the first semester of my senior year at Perkins.

I was seventeen, assertive, determinedly independent, the winner of a national high school wrestling title and as bored now by school as I was by most of the blind students. I was restlessly waiting to leap the wall.

In terms of my personal contacts I now skimmed the surface. Dad had virtually abandoned me. My sisters had gone from home. Mom, overprotective still, failed to understand my desire for freedom, a desire that dripped adrenaline into my bloodstream. I had almost lost touch with the Greaton Road gang. Friendships at

Perkins, notably with Ernie and Jerry, were essentially a comradeship of rebellion. Together we regarded rules as made only to be broken. We drank liquor, for instance, and smoked, not because we liked these minor vices but because we relished the risk of expulsion. We came close to expulsion the night we attempted to crawl through a sewer to the girls' dorm. If someone had not flushed the sewer when the citadel was all but breached, we might have updated the legendary rape of the Sabine women.

However, I was remembering something much more fragrant than the effluence that saturated us on that occasion. If the manufacturers of Chanel No. 5 need personal testimony as to its effect upon a seventeen-year-old schoolboy, they can call on me anytime.

Let me set the scene. The senior-class boys are being lined up in the school doctor's anteroom for physicals. Ernie and I have arrived late and are bouncing a basketball. A voice as crisply fresh and cool as a mountain spring reprimands us.

"Would you two please stop playing and pay attention."

So she is the one wearing the perfume. "Okay, miss," I respond. "We'll behave if you'll join us for the physical."

"Don't be obnoxious," says Chanel No. 5.

My mind vainly searches for repartee and then lamely I ask her name. It is Miss Francillon; she's a teacher trainee and a recent graduate of Smith College.

Ten days later, I am on duty at the candy concession of the senior class, and my nostrils suddenly flare to the scent of Chanel No. 5.

"Hi, Miss Francillon!"

"You guessed it was me?"

"ESP," I lie.

She buys two ice-cream cones, and as we lick them she asks me about my plans on leaving the school, what subjects especially interest me, that sort of thing. No specific plans, I tell her, but I presume I will go on to college. As to specialties, I am lousy in math but I enjoy literature, notably Tennessee Williams, Eugene O'Neill and Faulkner. As we exchange pleasantries I become acutely aware of her femininity. Her voice caresses my imagination. She suddenly says, "I like the books you like. Would it help if I read to you sometimes?"

I can think of nothing more attractive than being closeted with this cool, perfumed woman. I would not decline her offer to read me Socrates in Greek.

So it was that I set out on the exhilarating adventure of finding the first profound human relationship beyond my kin, classroom and street clan. Sometimes Hope Francillon would read to me in the library, sometimes on a campus bench, occasionally in fair weather on the riverbank. One day I mentioned that Peter Nero was giving a concert in Boston and Hope spoke rapturously about the jazz pianist.

"I'll take you," I said gallantly. "I'll ask my father to get tickets."

Dad did better than that. He sent a Cadillac limousine to pick us up at Perkins and take us to the theater. This was the first of a dozen similar Friday evenings. With Dad financing tickets and dinners, Hope and I went to the opera, to Symphony Hall to hear Beethoven's Fifth, to a marvelous performance of *Romeo and Juliet* by the Old Vic, to the Boston Pops, even to the ballet. She took me places too, to sites of historical interest, like Bunker Hill, where she explained the layout of the land where the colonists had fired the shots that started the War of Independence.

With Hope retelling the drama of the nation's founding, as we walked across once-bloodied turf and through rooms where men had plotted or stood patriots' trial, history emerged from the dust-dry textbooks to become a lively part of my heritage. When I sat with Hope in the theater, Shakespeare spoke directly to me down the long centuries; now his plays were no longer a classroom dirge for me, but throbbed with meter, tension.

In throwing wide the frontiers of culture, Hope became for me both heroine and first love. Yet I had not touched her, except in the necessary function of mobility. Unable to articulate my feelings, I felt as if our relationship were encompassed by a magic sphere as vulnerable as a soap bubble.

I yearned to take this lovely woman in my arms, to explore the flesh that radiated so much femininity. Yet stronger than this yearning was my fear that one embrace, one sensual intertwine of fingers would sever the sublime communion of two souls.

It is common practice to mock first love, to dismiss it in the same breath with pubescent pimples. But no one who mocks my own enchanted experience can understand my feelings; he is not my friend. Although disaster was soon to follow, Hope possesses a corner of my heart forever hers.

First warning of the trouble that lay ahead came from my English teacher, Mr. Ackerman. He asked me to stay behind one day at the end of class. When we were alone, he cautioned, "Tom, you can't win this chess game."

"Chess game? Win? I don't know what you mean."

"I think you do," said Mr. Ackerman. "And so does Miss Francillon."

My shock was quickly replaced by cold, gray anger. I protested in a deluge of adjectives that the game he spoke of was played entirely in the open, that Hope gave me her time and patience only to help me expand my world. I protested with the fury of innocence.

When my outburst subsided, Mr. Ackerman expressed his sympathy but warned me that there were members of the administration who would not be as tolerant as he. That evening I reported to Hope the gist of the alarming and incredible exchange. She was hardly less shocked than I but recognized that we had to be discreet. We decided to meet from now on only on weekends. She continued to take me to theaters, concerts and places of interest, but now Dad's rented limousine picked us up at home.

For the next four months Hope and I did not speak to each other at all on campus. At times I singled out her perfume. I knew she watched me rehearse the role of Matt in a school production of *The Fantasticks*. The musical is about a boy (Matt) and a girl (Luisa) whose parents try to force them together, but because they are too immature the contrived romance fails. Matt then has various adventures around the world and returns to discover that Luisa is in fact the one he truly loves.

On the evening of the first public performance I sent Hope a bouquet of roses and told her in a brief note that what success I had had was due to her—that she had given me confidence and understanding of the role. I suggested that the story of the play might yet parallel our own.

Later that night, I was still flushed with success over my first lead role when Hope telephoned me from her dorm. She congratulated me and thanked me for the roses.

"A lovely, lovely gesture," she said, "but your stage triumph, Tommy, has been all the reward I need. I'm just so happy that I could be of help to a person like you. You've shown me that the handicapped can live normal lives. That's why I came here, Tommy, that's why I'm at Perkins."

The phone clicked. "Are you still there?" I asked.

"Still here," said Hope.

"Sounded as though someone picked up an extension phone," I said.

"No need to worry," she replied.

"Then I want to tell you ... that I love you," I stammered.

She was silent for some seconds and then said, "Tommy, you mustn't say that. It's not the right time, not the right place."

"You don't want me to tell the truth?"

"It's too early for you to know this truth."

"I just know that I love you," I said.

Another moment of silence and then she whispered, "I care for you too, Tommy, very, very much. But we can't talk like this, not now—please."

I heard her put down the receiver. I held on to the instrument a moment longer and then heard a second click. I was soon to understand its significance.

Next morning I was summoned from class to the office of Dr. Solomon Wise, the dean of Perkins. No sooner had I entered the plush office than I picked up the scent of Chanel No. 5. Hope was here!

Dr. Wise was an elderly graduate of England's Cambridge University. He still spoke in transatlantic idiom and accent. His main responsibility was to activate the faculty, but he spent most of his time traveling all over to raise funds for the school. When in his office, he was consulted only on major issues of policy. I could not begin to conceive what business he might have with me.

"Ah, Mr. Sullivan," he huffed, "please be seated." It was characteristic of Dr. Wise's pomposity that he addressed senior students as mister or miss.

Then the first flash of trouble. "We have here a distasteful business, I'm afraid. I should rightly begin by apologizing to you, Mr. Sullivan."

"For what?" I asked.

Dr. Wise enjoyed his pauses. A ridiculously loud wall clock ticked off five seconds.

"For failing to protect you from a member of the faculty."

That was it! Here was the reason why Hope was sitting two paces away from me. There was a fourth person in the room, someone cracking knuckles by the window. I wondered who it was. My heart was beginning to thump. Dr. Wise was obviously waiting for me to respond but it was Hope who interjected. Her voice was cool.

"I would like to know what this is all about," she said. "My Braille class has no teacher."

Dr. Wise cleared his throat. "We will not keep you longer than necessary, Miss Francillon. Mr. Haring and I felt it prudent that both of you should be present." It was my counselor, Mr. Haring, who was cracking his knuckles. At least he was an ally. I had told him all about my relationship with Hope. He knew how innocent it was.

Dr. Wise continued. "I want to say formally on behalf of Perkins School, Mr. Sullivan, that we are deeply sorry that we have not been able to protect you from the—er—the provocative behavior of this young lady member of the faculty."

If he had fired a shot or used four-letter words he could not have amazed me more. It was so absurd I nearly started to laugh, but caught myself when I heard Hope burst into tears. It was only then that I fully realized what Dr. Wise was saying. He had just described the woman I worshiped as a hustler. The rest of the meeting in that overfurnished, overheated office is now a confusion of memories. I remember Hope standing against the desk, thumping her fist against the walnut as she sobbed out her innocence. I remember hearing her declare why she had come to Perkins, how she had hated the leering treatment she had always encountered and had decided to give her life to a worthwhile career and a cause, to helping people who desperately needed help.

I remember facing my counselor and appealing to

him to admit what he knew—that my relationship with Hope had been physically pure. Mr. Haring knew that the love I had for Hope was the most wonderful thing that had happened to me; that this experience was being distorted by a hideous, malicious lie. But Mr. Haring responded by saying that there was "reason to believe" the relationship had "gone beyond propriety." When I had demanded to know the basis of this grotesque accusation, he puffed about a "reliable report" made to him the previous night. I at once connected this remark with the mysterious clicks on the phone.

I can still hear that noisy clock, which seemed to be ticking away my life. Crushed, bitter and humiliated, Hope and I then stood side by side at the walnut desk. She was convulsed by sobs; I was shaking with fury.

Then Dr. Solomon Wise pronounced his verdict. "Miss Francillon, Mr. Sullivan, you will not see each other again socially. I will want your solemn pledge on this. If you refuse to comply, you leave us no choice but to expel you both from the school."

"I won't!" I yelled at him.

Hope turned and held my upper arms. "No, Tom, you have to graduate. You've got to make a future for yourself. Don't worry about me; my future's not important. I can always teach sighted children. I can . . ."

She broke down again. Dr. Solomon Wise retreated a few inches and cleared his throat once more.

"Now, now! We are not unjust here at Perkins. We're anxious to do the right thing for the school. We are not trying to ruin you. We will give you until Monday to make your promise. But in fairness I should warn you, Miss Francillon, that if you do not see things our way, I personally will see that no handicapped child will again be placed in your charge, not at Perkins, not anywhere."

As we left Dr. Wise's office, both of us were too emotionally drained to fire off any Parthian shots. As we separated in the corridor, Hope whispered, "Meet me at the river at eight tonight."

I knew exactly where but not what she meant. Our rendezvous was the bench where we had often sat together all alone, listening to the river. It was where she had read aloud to me often.

Her perfume was on the chill April air when I arrived. She immediately took me in her arms and kissed me—not a tender kiss, not the kiss I had expected, but prolonged and predatory, savage with teeth and tongue. She pulled my hands inside her coat. She was naked.

She said, "They called me a whore; then I'll be a whore."

Her voice was acid hard; no longer the fresh cool voice I had grown to love. As we rolled on the dew-wet grass of the riverbank, the fragile sphere that had encompassed us was smashed, splintering like a wineglass dropped on concrete. When her fingers clawed into my back I realized she was not making a gift of her body to Tom Sullivan but was physically attacking the system and the people who had wrenched from her heart the selflessness, the sense of dedication that had brought her to the school.

Sexually satiated, we wept. Tears met tears and seemed to meld with the river at our feet. The magic of our former love and communion was gone.

A long time later I met Hope Francillon again. She was not wearing Chanel No. 5 anymore, but an overpowering cheap perfume. She had married twice, both times unhappily. Her conversation now seemed trite and silly to me. The young woman of compassion I had known had become a hardened shell. Perhaps one day someone will answer for having destroyed a lovely soul. Maybe it wasn't destroyed. I still cherish my memories of Hope and pray her fantastic capacity to give has not been totally lost.

8. Faith and Fresh Fervor

Three months after the traumatic experiences in the office of Dr. Wise and on the riverbank, I was graduated from Perkins. I had won scholarships from both Harvard and Yale and fresh wrestling titles. I had sung under Fiedler's baton for President Johnson. Physically I was now in my prime, hard-muscled, coordinated, but my heart had taken such a battering that I had built up, brick by brick, a wall of cynicism and bitterness around me.

Without emotional feeling toward any human being (except contempt) and without desire to search for my life's meaning, I drifted in self-pitying gloom, which my mother feared might be suicidal. She consulted the parish priest, who came hot-foot to visit me. We held a desultory and boring philosophical exchange, and to get rid of him I flippantly agreed to take a summer job as a counselor to underprivileged boys at Camp Cathedral, near Freetown, Massachusetts.

In my then current frame of mind, I considered myself eminently unsuited for the work, but the old priest was wiser than I had recognized in understanding that the best therapy for my almost total absorption in myself was to do something worthwhile for someone else. Arriving at the summer camp, I was given the titles of music director and wrestling coach. I lived with the young Catholic seminarians who staffed the place.

Among the seminarians was a short, rotund intellectual who introduced himself as Bill Burns. I had no inkling that this Friar Tuck (for so I always think of him) was to play a major role in the story of my life. He had been in a poker game and lost badly. I asked him why.

83

"Because," he said, "I have a face too honest and I cannot bluff."

I have never read a valid analysis of what constitutes friendship; why it is that two people who seem to have nothing in common, who are separated, perhaps, by age, culture, background and interests, can together find warm comradeship.

Physically Bill and I were as different as Laurel from Hardy. Mentally we found common ground but spiritually again we diverged. He was a man humbly in quest of God, while I had by that time convinced myself that God was a crutch for the weakling. Yet our friendship was instant and blossomed daily.

Bill sensed my deep depression yet did not probe its cause—not until I was ready to speak of it myself. The camp days were full, and in the evenings when the boys had gone to bed Bill joined me at the lake shore. It was I, not Bill, who first shifted our conversation from trivialities to the more personal. Because I was genuinely curious, I asked how a man of his intellectual competence could possibly accept the teachings of the Church. He did not answer immediately, and for a while we listened to the crickets and the frogs. Then to my surprise he confessed that he was plagued by doubts.

I had anticipated his heated defense of the Church's doctrine and had already marshaled arguments for apostasy and atheism. But maybe because I enjoyed debate, I found myself not playing the devil's advocate but championing the Sermon on the Mount. I had not been to confession or Mass in three years, and I was as painfully limp in argument as in exegesis.

Bill heard me through and laughed infectiously. "I suspect," he said, "that the blind is trying to lead the blind and that both of us are in danger of falling into the lake."

I laughed too, and then Bill suggested that the next

evening if might do us both good if we reexamined the lives of those who had fumbled their way from dark doubts to blazing faith.

So there began a series of such evenings that were to last through most of the summer, evenings in which Bill and I studied the lives of the saints and the source of their faith.

Armed with mosquito repellent and a hurricane lamp, we would go to an isolated place on the lake shore and, with our backs against a tree trunk, he would read to me in a resonant voice.

In reading *The Confessions of Saint Augustine*, I found myself in a time machine, as it were, transported to the fourth century and identifying closely with a young student who stole for the sake of stealing, who chased women and "could not distinguish the white light of love from the fog of lust," who boasted of questionable exploits—"the viler the exploits, the louder the boasting."

Bill took on for me the role of Bishop Ambrose, the man of God who received Augustine as a brother, and as Augustine came to love and respect his "teacher of truth," so I deepened my affection and respect for Bill.

It was all so relevant to my situation. Augustine had confessed that he was "all hot for honors, money and esteem," but in the pursuit of these he had suffered bitter disappointments. By the time we reached the point of Augustine's mystical conversion, I found myself shifting in low gear from atheism to agnosticism and into a lukewarm faith.

I was elated by the life of Saint Francis of Assisi, initially because of his love of nature. As a child I had heard the saint's story from my mother, but Bill gave fresh meaning to the life of the "gentlest and most humble of men." Bill knew the Prayer of Saint Francis by heart. He snapped the book shut, swatted a mosquito and began to recite the prayer, accompanied by an orchestra of croaking frogs and chirruping crickets.

> "Lord, make me an instrument of Your peace.
> Where there is hatred may I bring love;
> Where there is malice may I bring pardon;
> Where there is discord may I bring harmony;
> Where there is error may I bring truth;
> Where there is doubt may I bring faith;
> Where there is despair may I bring hope;
> Where there is darkness may I bring Your light;
> Where there is sadness may I bring joy."

Bill paused to allow the crickets and frogs a triumphant crescendo and a night bird to twitter somewhere behind us in the forest. The sound effects could not have been better staged as Bill concluded the Franciscan prayer:

> "Oh, Master, may I seek not so much to be
>   comforted as to comfort,
> To be understood as to understand,
> To be loved as to love,
> For it is in giving that we receive,
> It is in forgiving that we shall be forgiven. . . ."

In the strange beauty of this moment I felt a marvelous sense of joy and freedom. The bitterness I had experienced at Perkins, especially toward those who had destroyed the first deep love I had felt for anyone, seemed to fall away like a heavy load released from the shoulders. If this was religion, then I bought it. If this was the food of faith, then I hungered for it.

Through the following evenings of high summer we read excerpts from Saint Thomas Aquinas, including the exquisite part of the *Summa* on the essence of love.

One evening we went out in a rowboat on the lake

and I told Bill about my life and longings, about the
sublime and devastating experiences with Hope Francillon, about my fears and uncertainty concerning my
future. I finished by saying I believed I had refound a
faith in God. I thanked him for giving me so much.

Bill shipped he oars and said, "Tom, the giving has
flowed the other way in equal measure. When we first
met I told you of my doubts. If I had told the full truth
I would have said that I planned to quit the seminary.
You have shown me that my work is in the Church.
I'm now resolved to take my vows."

Bill made his own prophecy for my future—or was
it just a hope, because he wisely did not back it with a
wager. Thinking his thoughts aloud, he envisioned
Tom Sullivan as a philosopher in the age of science, as
one empowered or inspired to influence his own generation. He saw the new renaissance of youth as the only
hope of holding back the black tide of cynicism and
materialism. He placed me in the renaissance's van-
guard and refused to retract when I rocked the boat
with laughter.

What Bill did convince me of, however, as we sat in
a rowboat in the middle of a lake at midnight (and
astride, so he told me, a moonbeam), was that I should
turn down my scholarships for both Harvard and Yale
and attend, at least for a year or two, Providence College, the Catholic university in Rhode Island.

My Perkins gloom and sadness now quite dissipated
by frank and cheerful friendship, I looked forward to
fresh challenges and fortunes. With new-found faith,
my hopes were crusader high that I might even
reconcile my parents.

The reconciliation nearly happened over a camp dinner. I had invited Mom and Dad to come to camp and
talk over my plans for Providence. I introduced them
to Bill and, with the zeal of a new convert, told them
of my spiritual adventures. I was ready for Dad's sar-

donic laughter and not put out at all when he told Bill
that he, Dad, had already made his pact to get past the
pearly gates. Dad was quite ready, he said with a
belch, to give Saint Peter 40 percent of his nightclub.

Unshockable and unshocked—hence his strength
with people—Bill spoke with humanity and humor of
life and the basic needs of the common man. The dinner lasted longer than Dad's supply of beer. I didn't
remember Dad's ever before being interested in any
discussion of the ancient verities. Once again I wished
that the get-together would help reestablish my
parents' domestic bliss; that because of it Dad would
find inspired ways of sorting out the tangle of his life;
that Mom would defrost her heart with forgiveness.
But just as my earlier hopes had been stifled, so again
the unfolding of my parents' lives did not conform to
my most ardent expectations.

Impoverished by his enormous tax assessment, Dad
had just sold the twenty-two-room house in Milton.
Mom had had to retreat to lace-curtain living in a
modest Milton house. It was from this simple home
that Dad had picked Mom up and brought her to
Camp Cathedral; and it was to this home that Mom
would return—alone.

But before they left, my parents nodded their warm
approval to my plans to go to Providence, and two
days later Bill and I took camp leave and made an appointment with the dean.

No blind student had ever been entered for Providence, and the dean was more than reluctant to en-
roll me. It was Bill who persuaded him. He talked in
glowing terms of my work with the boys at camp. He
portrayed me as a Samson when he spoke of sport. If I
were ever to live up to his tribute to my musical talent,
then a world looking for the next Beethoven should be
trampling a path to my door.

The Sullivans enjoying a casual lunch.

Tom at the piano.

Tom on horseback.

Tom and Patty enjoy a quiet evening at home by the fire.

Traveling through life together.

In the movie IF YOU CAN SEE WHAT I HEAR, Marc Singer plays Tom Sullivan and Shari Belafonte Harper is Heather Johnson, a fellow student with whom Tom becomes involved.

Tom (Marc Singer) and his father, "Porky" Sullivan (Douglas Campbell), toss darts in his father's bar.

Determined to excel in sports, Tom takes up wrestling.

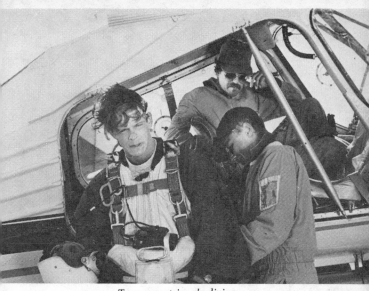

Tom even tries skydiving.

Tom and his friend, Tom Sly (R. H. Thomson), are stopped by the police after a wild session of "blind" driving.

Patty Steffan (Sarah Torgov) places the tee for Tom in a golf game.

So in a mix-up of architectural blueprints, as it were, Camp Cathedral turned out to be a bridge from heartbreak to hilarity, from days of deepest hurt to peaks of youthful joy.

9. Comradeship and a Coup d'état

There were three good reasons why I did not leave Providence College within a month. The first was my fumbling new-found faith that there was "Someone out there" who really cared for me. The second reason was Bill, who came to see me at a point of crisis. The third was a lanky, loose-limbed student who bore the unlikely Dickensian name Tom Sly.

On a Sunday in mid-September, 1965, my parents drove me down to Providence. I was filled with apprehension. For the first time in my life I would be a complete stranger in a strange land. There was not one name I knew among the 2,600 students. The geography of the campus was as unknown to me as America was to Columbus when he set out from Spain. I had no idea how to study, for I had neither Braille books nor records. The thought of even finding my way to the dorm bathroom terrified me. What would happen if I was "caught short" and there were no students around to show me the way?

The sighted person would find it difficult if not impossible to comprehend the fears that seized and froze me when I went to the school cafeteria for supper on that first evening. I heard a clatter of trays and conversation like a wave sweeping over a pebbled beach. My plate and mug were filled, but how and where to find a table? Before a student took my arm I had crashed into half a dozen chairs and tables and was the butt of curses as coffee was spilled ("What the hell?" . . . "You clumsy son of a bitch"), followed by embarrassed apologies when it was noticed I was blind.

Next morning, how to find the hall for freshman registration and orientation? Unlike the Perkins campus, which was designed to facilitate its students' mobility, Providence seemed designed to confuse, bruise and destroy. Classroom doors would suddenly fly open and knock me down. My nose and lips were slashed by collisions with fire extinguishers suspended at corridor corners, my knees swollen from colliding with sidewalk hydrants.

Up to now I had not experienced failure. I had left Perkins at the top of the totem pole—an athlete with a national title and a reputation for high spirits. Here I was at the bottom of the heap, friendless and missing half my classes because I could not find my way. When a student or member of the faculty saw my cane probing for doors and took my arm, I too often resented his patronage.

In order to be able to study the lectures, I had bought a tape recorder, not the cassette kind—these had not yet been marketed—but one of the earlier clumsy prototypes, which required tape-threading into spools. When recording lectures, I frequently discovered that I had twisted the tape or threaded it incorrectly. A minute later I would find yards of tape tangled about my feet. I began to wallow in self-pity. One evening, alone in my dorm and hungry (because there was no one around to take me to the cafeteria), I heard a familiar voice down the corridor. Bill had unexpectedly arrived to check up on me. I embraced him and poured out my sorrows. I was quitting Providence, I told him. It was hopeless to go on. I was missing classes; I couldn't find readers. There was no one on the campus who seemed to give a damn. I raised the cuffs of my pants and showed Bill the welts and bruises on my legs. I bundled the twisted tape onto his knees.

"I'm just a goddamned blind kid," I whined. "I thought I could fight my way out of the snake pit of blindness, but now I know that I can't. I'm gonna have

to spend the rest of my life weaving baskets or whatever. Who the hell said I could make it in the sighted
world? You know damned well I can't. You know I
haven't got a chance. Why was I born blind? Go on,
answer that one. It'd been better if I'd been born
Mongolian or a village idiot. Then I wouldn't have to
think. I wouldn't have ambition. They could have given
me a tin mug and a busy street corner and I'd have
been reasonably happy. It's people like you who've
made my life a hell. You've tried to make me reach for
the impossible. I'm blind, don't you understand that,
Bill? I'm blind! Blind! Blind!"

I was panting with rage and frustration. My nails
were cutting my palms.

Bill heard me through without interruption and then
said savagely, "Okay, Sullivan, you gutless S.O.B., get
out of here. Quit. I misread your character up at Camp
Cathedral. I'm the fool. You're just a flabby, knock-
kneed little bastard after all. I'll help you pack and
drive you home to Mama."

Although his was hardly the language of a semi-
narian, Bill knew his psychology and knew me well
enough to guess how I would react. Had he preached
to me at that moment, had he pressed his fingers together and talked of God, martydom and duty, I
would have left that night for Boston. When I yelled
back abuse, he knew he had won the battle.

Yet winning one battle is not to win a war. A long
and dismal week after the evening with Bill, I began to
droop again and drowned my sorrows in a pint of
bourbon. Next morning, with temples a-throb and the
taste of burning tennis shoes on my tongue, I groped
my way to the dorm showers. Cold water provided
some relief, but then I dropped the soap and lost it at
my feet. My fingers were fumbling over slippery tiles
when the deepest voice I'd ever heard inquired,
"What's wrong with you?"

"The soap," I groaned. "Where the hell?"

"Must have been some party," said the voice, in bottom G. "It's at your heel. You blind or something?"

" 'S'matter of fact, I am," I said and straightened up.

I was of course used to incidents like this, generally followed at once by stuttered apologies: "Excuse me . . . terribly sorry . . . I didn't realize. . . ." But the bass voice only grunted and a moment later the soap was pushed into my hands.

While we toweled ourselves dry we exchanged names. "Tom Sly," he said, and the voice now seemed to come from the ceiling. He had to be at least six foot five, I thought, and to weigh two hundred fifty pounds. I was wrong about the weight. As soon as he offered an elbow to lead me back to my room, I realized Tom was yardstick thin.

So in stark nakedness there began a David and Jonathan friendship, the richest male friendship of my life. How do I accurately describe Tom Sly? I've never seen his face, of course. I know he wears glasses, that he favors old tweed sports coats with leather at the elbows. I know he can empty a tankard of beer down his long neck in two and a half seconds. With a humor as dry as the Mojave Desert, he is the most even-tempered man I've ever met. Suffice it to say at this point that my love for this ungainly, gregarious and gallant man is a love for all seasons.

In our friendship there was not the least flavor of saccharine. On the contrary, it was from its outset a comradeship of boisterous rivalry, and when one of us hit the dirt the other roared with laughter.

An incident two weeks after our first meeting will reveal the nature of our fraternal bond. I was dressing for a freshman dance when Tom shuffled into my room. He made some observation about my being "late as usual" and then, as he sat on the edge of my bed, he asked flatly, "I'm your friend, right?"

"I invoke the Fifth Amendment," I replied.

"No, seriously," said Tom in earnest. "You won't get mad at me if I tell you something?"

"Probably," I said.

"You've got your socks on the wrong feet."

"Get out of here," I yelled.

"Okay—only trying to be helpful." He walked to the door. "Just don't want you to look like an idiot, that's all."

I weakened a fraction. "What d'ya mean—socks on the wrong feet?"

"Doesn't matter," he said. "Not my business."

He had almost caught me—but not quite.

"You can't put socks on the wrong feet!" I protested.

He paused now. It was superbly done. Then he came back to the bed and put his bony hands on my shoulders.

"Look," he said almost tenderly, "do you really think I'd kid you on a thing like this? Now, if I had told you you were black, you'd have known I was kidding. I guess no one has ever had the guts to tell you about your socks. I noticed them yesterday."

I now imagined myself at the dance, stretching out my legs and looking like a clown. Tom Sly's hook was in my throat and he felt the tug on the line. He played me like a veteran angler.

His words were slow, as if he were talking to a child. "There's a left and right arm for your shirt sleeves?"

"Yes."

"When you put your pants on, same thing, right?"

"Uh-huh."

"Ever put your shoes on the wrong way round?"

"No."

"Well, there's a left and a right sock."

"How—how do I know which is which?"

"Same way you feel your shoes—with your big toes."

For the next half hour, with Tom making sympathetic noises, I tried to get the big-toe feel of a left and a right sock. After one series of four "losses" when I was frantic with frustration, he allowed me three consecutive "wins." Then he parodied the *My Fair Lady* song, "I think he's got it! I think he's got it!"

We were late for the dance, but for my comfort I assumed that I was sartorially turned out well—from head to toe.

Tom Sly had not finished with me yet. I was dancing the Watusi with a girl who hardly spoke English. I imagined I was performing pretty well. Suddenly Tom's voice drowned out the band.

"Where's your partner?" he asked.

"Get out of my way," I shouted.

"Your girl's on the other side of the room," he said. "Doesn't look too good, but you're dancing with me."

I went home to Boston that weekend and immediately rebuked my mother. "Why didn't you ever tell me that there's a left and a right sock?"

Mom was close to tears as she protested. "Those horrible boys must be giving you a bad time."

That Sunday evening when I returned to Providence, I was bent on vengeance. When Tom ambled into my room, a joke on his lips, I turned out the light. His advantage lost in the darkness, he was easily pillow-thumped to the floor. Twisting Tom's arm behind his back, I made him squeal for mercy. I gave his arm a final twist, a degree short of fracture. He never asked why I had attacked him, but he never referred to my socks again!

On Saint Patrick's Day Tom Sly and I found ourselves on the same side. In making the rounds of pubs, we ran completely out of money and decided to sing for our supper. Tom borrowed a guitar, which he played very badly, and I went into a slurring rendition of "Danny Boy." I don't know who it was who objected (possibly the proprietor) or who hit Tom in the solar plexus. As Tom fell over me, I reached out and grabbed his assailant in a wrestling hold, hurling him across the bar. The sound of broken bottles persuaded me I had won a victory. But the whole bar then exploded into a melee of the thudding fists and flying glasses. Swinging my arms wildly, I cut my knuckles on someone's teeth. The teeth belonged to a policeman.

I phoned Dad from jail. He too had been celebrating Ireland's patron saint. He gloated over my story of the Irish donnybrook and could not have been more pleased that I had ended up behind bars.

"Ireland's proud of ye tonight, me boy. Did yer hit the bastards good?"

His storm of laughter almost fused the phone. Then he asked me how much cash I needed. Two hours later Dad sent the three-hundred-dollar bail bond to our jail.

On a November evening in 1965, large areas of the East Coast were plunged into darkness by the most serious electric power failure in the nation's history. "The Night the Lights Went Out" was grist to comedians. The failure trapped millions in offices, on stalled trains and in elevators stuck between floors.

The chaos at Providence College was typical. Students were unable to find their way to dining rooms, and those few who succeeded fumbled for cold, unidentifiable food. For me the blackout was marvelous. I enormously enjoyed the helplessness of my sighted friends, especially of Tom Sly, whom I discovered bundled up in blankets in his room.

"Of course you understand what this is all about," I said.

"What the hell?" came a grunt from the bed.

"It's been top secret up to now," I said flatly, "but I guess it's time to disclose the facts."

"Shoot," he said listlessly.

"The fact is that we blind people have been planning this blackout for a long time. We are taking over."

Tom's response was very rude indeed. Then he slapped his thigh and urged me with unexpected enthusiasm to tell the campus of the *coup d'état*.

Because Tom was currently involved in the election of class officers, he temporarily possessed a portable bullhorn. Armed with this, we walked to the center of the campus. I switched on the bullhorn and my voice thundered into the darkness.

"Gentlemen, your attention, please. Your attention, please." My voice echoed back from the walls of the dormitories. "It can now be revealed why you have been plunged into darkness." I paused for dramatic impact. I heard windows and doors opening and many shuffling feet. I raised the bullhorn to my mouth again.

"You have heard of the suppressed people. You know about the Jews and Negroes. We, the blind people of the earth, have been a suppressed minority for too long. We are striking back. We are taking over the earth. In Washington my blind comrades have already seized the White House, the Capitol and the Pentagon. I am now in control of this campus. I, Tom Sullivan, was sent here for this special task."

More doors were banging, more windows opening. The crowd around me was thickening and murmuring.

"Our dictatorship will be benevolent," I bellowed. "We will teach you to use your ears. As the darkness smothers you, we will teach you to use your hands. We will sharpen your sense of touch. You have nothing to fear as long as you are obedient to your new masters."

The applause from several hundred students was intoxicating.

"Do you understand these great truths?" I yelled.

"We understand. We are with you," came the crowd's response.

"Are you sorry for your suppression of the blind people?" I asked.

"We are sorry," shouted the crowd.

"Do you accept me, Thomas J. Sullivan, as your undisputed leader?"

"You are our leader. Hail Sullivan! Hail Sullivan!" came the reply.

By now the bullhorn had brought out almost everyone on campus within range of my voice. For the benefit of newcomers I repeated the gist of my address. Over the uproar of "hails" I sternly warned against counter-revolutionary measures that might be attempted at sunrise. I listed in detail the monstrous crimes against the world's blind people and cautioned that a Braille book had been kept listing the major criminals.

It was only because the bullhorn developed an uncontrollable whistle that I switched it off and went to bed. Led by the bass voice of Tom Sly, intermittent cries of "Hail Tom Sullivan!" lulled me to sleep.

As the blackout lasted only six hours, my coup d'état may be marked down as the shortest in history.

After "The Night the Lights Went Out," I reveled in campus popularity, but Tom was always alert for a chance to deflate my ego. One evening when I went to the gym for a workout, I couldn't understand why my arrival should evoke ribald laughter. Although Tom never admitted doing it, I'm sure it was he who had scrawled slogans in bold letters across my shorts—slogans like: "Jeannie's been here!" and "Save our environment from the Great Polluter!" and "Danger! The blind have V.D.!"

Boisterous occasions such as these were the feature of my special friendship with Tom Sly but other friendships blossomed too. Within my inner circle was Phil Souza, a varsity hocky player whose prowess and charm had entrapped a very attractive girl, Marie Morin (who later became his wife).

Under the stern and watchful eye of the Dean of Discipline, it was difficult to smuggle a girl into a monastic dormitory. Phil approached me one evening with his problem. Would I bring Marie to the dorm on a pretext that she was one of my team of readers? I objected that there was too much risk in this deception, as all my readers were known and approved. On learning from Phil that Marie was under five feet tall and weighed less than one hundred pounds, I facetiously volunteered to sneak her to home ground in his hockey bag. Phil at once accepted the offer.

With the girl zipped up in the bag, and with the bag slung across my shoulder, I entered the dorm elevator. By the unhappiest of coincidences, the Dean of Discipline, Father Raymond St. George, entered too.

"Ah! Mr. Sullivan," said the dean's voice, "I truly had not heard that you played hocky."

"Me? Hockey? Oh, yes, Father. I'm giving it a try." The truth was that I had never even put on ice skates in my life.

I heard the dean press the elevator button. "Very remarkable. Don't you find some difficulty in following the puck?"

The elevator was now moving. "Some difficulty, but I'm getting the hang of it."

The dean got out on the second floor. He held back the doors. "I'd like to see you play. I really would. What about tomorrow evening, say, at eight o'clock?"

Those who have skated will understand the misery of trying to learn the skill in twenty-four hours. Although Phil Souza was my coach, he failed to protect my backside from hitting the ice. My calves and ankles were seared with pain. I was a wreck by the time Father St. George appeared. For perhaps five minutes he watched me wobble about the ice like an elderly woman with rheumatoid arthritis. When I crashed into the boards, he left without comment, overcome, presumably, by the pathos of the scene. Phil may have been telling the truth in claiming he saw tears glisten on the dean's lined and weathered cheeks.

Because Tom Sly, Phil Souza and my other friends accepted me now as one of themselves, my self-confidence was boosted, and doubly so when I was invited with six hundred signatures to be president of the freshman class. While acknowledging the honor, I turned the invitation down because my days were too crowded. I was determined to do well academically and I had started a wrestling program. Providence had never had a wrestling team, but within a year we beat Brown University, Holy Cross and Boston College. It was during this period, as both competitor and coach, that I won the New England A.A.U. championship.

Blindness was now less a handicap than a nuisance in my resolve to live a full and exuberant student life.

Tom Sly and I were taking the same courses—English, education and psychology. Our rivalry was extended to the classroom. In our sophomore year I just beat him to the wire, heading the class with straight A's.

Socially, in sport and academically, life surged forward on a spring tide of mirth and student escapades. Yet in one area I wallowed in stagnation.

At Camp Cathedral I had cautiously but with genuine intent felt my way toward an adventure of the spirit. For the first time in my life I had been pointed to a faith, at least to one vastly more satisfying than confession, Mass and enforced listening to ponderous homilies in marble halls. With Bill's help I had been able to separate ecclesiastical theology from the buoyant, effervescent free questing of a youthful soul for life's meaning. In the lives of Augustine, Aquinas and Francis of Assisi I had come to comprehend, at least in part, the innate desire in every human being to find a

higher cause than the daily rat race for profit, fame
and pleasure.

What had captured my imagination on the lake of
Camp Cathedral was the sense of being unfettered by
priestly rule and papal precept. The faith in which I'd
taken faltering steps seduced me with its sweet simplic-
ity, the purest ethics of the Testament.

When Bill and I had talked of the deep yearnings of
the human heart, I recognized that it is not what a man
says that matters, but how he lives—that men who
speak as angels yet have not love are "as sounding
brass or a tinkling cymbal."

After taking that first cool, refreshing breath of understanding, I found myself at Providence being smothered in a fog of dogma, incantations and regimented in-
terpretations.

"Forbear to judge, for we are sinners all," said
Shakespeare, and I have no intention of condemning
the Dominican priests who saw themselves as my spiritual advisers. I merely state as fact that their rigid
rules gave me at first a spiritual wheeze and then intellectual bronchitis. The point was reached where I
could inhale no more.

The incident of rejection of Dominican theology was
trifling, but the result was spiritual disaster. Tom Sly
and I were roughhousing with a third student, Joe, who
we thought had been obnoxious. Without malice, we
dangled Joe by his toes outside a second-story window
of McDermott Hall. Joe's loud protests brought a particularly officious priest to his rescue. We heaved Joe
back inside the room, and the priest, quivering with
rage, accused us of three grievous sins.

"You have committed a felony against a fellow
man," he spluttered. "You have transgressed the right
of a fellow man to submit himself to choice." Then,
sniffing our breath, the priest added, "And I suspect
you have been sinning against temperance."

Certainly Tom Sly and I were guilty of student stupidity, but to have equated this stupidity with theologi-
cal felonies was so asinine that even Joe was amused.
Perhaps Tom and I should have laughed too. Instead
we walked to a grotto on the campus and there
resolved that the dogma of the cloisters was not for us.
In so resolving, I did not reject my belief in God nor
my obligation to develop sympathy for my fellow men.
But now on Sunday mornings, when the bells summoned me to Mass, I slept on. Tom claimed I always
snored.

Does it sound ridiculous (if not sacrilegious) to say
that I saw Christ in the lanky figure of Tom Sly? If I
have not painted Tom as kin to Goofy, then my
portrait is a poor one. Yet at the same time Tom must
be seen as a Renaissance man, a man of truth and incredible compassion within the framework of the human beast. It was Tom who by nature gave without
asking or expecting anything in return, who made my
two years at Providence a period of accelerating joy.

During our summer vacation we camped (illegally)
on an island bird sanctuary, about four hundred yards
off Cotuit on the Cape Cod coast. We studied there together and perhaps because of my drive and mental
facility he worked harder than he would have had he
been alone.

On that island we slept under pup tents and lived
largely off clams, which I dug up, and lobster, which
Tom dived for. We pooled what little money we had
and, when needing a change in diet, rowed across to
the mainland for groceries. We had a common love of
music and a portable record player to help satisfy it,
but the memories I relish most are the languid evenings
when we discussed with gravity or with light hearts—
but always with total honesty—our concerns about life,
its mysteries, opportunities and purpose. Our dialogue
would shift tangentially to ribald jest, perhaps, or to

identifying bird song. Although neither poet nor artist by standard definition, Tom was unconsciously both as he attempted to articulate to me, who had never seen, the beauty of a sunset across a stretch of water, the color of a wild flower, the design of driftwood or the pattern of a shell.

After our two years at Providence, there came the day when we parted. Tom had decided to study for a year in Europe and I to go on to Harvard. I confess that when we said farewell and went our separate ways, I wept.

10. Hermit's Cell Off Harvard Square

Harvard spells out disaster in my mind, and in counting off the major errors in my life I mark my going there as number one. But that's not quite true. If I had not gone to Harvard I would not have met Patricia; there would have been no daughter Blythe, no Tommy Junior. Maybe it's true we have to stagger through the coldest, darkest valleys before we reach the sunsplashed plains. Perhaps we have to smell brimstone before we reach the Elysian Fields.

How strangely merciful is remembrance. It blankets our unhappiest memories even as it brings to the forefront of recollection the most ecstatic moments. I find myself reluctant to retrace in proper order the footprints of my journey. I'm impatient now to leap ahead, to find my next companionship, to tell the story of a girl, a woman, lovely and of gentle ways, for whom I would not exchange all treasure, all trophies, all applause.

Yet if this autobiography is to have validity I must not now recoil, but must speak, for instance, of the September morning of 1967 when I was twenty and when I was allocated a room in Section R of Harvard's Lowell House. I was to share this room with Cecil, whose father's name is in the Social Register.

Cecil and the seven other juniors in Section R had known each other for a year or more and, finding common interest in affluence and social status, had elected to live together. Tom Sullivan intruded on their closed and comfortable world.

The walls between the suites were thin. As I made my bed I could distinctly hear a conversation in the room next door. Cecil's reedy voice was raised in protest.

"Why the hell should I have to share a room with a goddamned blind kid?" he was saying.

Another student, later identified as Oliver, responded with a sneer, "For the good of your soul, you jerk."

"I thought we had the right of choice here," whined Cecil.

"Moan to President Pusey, not me," said Oliver.

"I plan to," said Cecil. "I'll be spending half my time mothering this kid."

The exchange behind the suite's partition continued along these lines until I heard Cecil and Oliver pacing out the room, calculating where to squeeze in another bed. A moment more, and Cecil appeared at my door with an oily greeting and an offer to do anything he could to help. He did indeed assist me in tucking in a blanket, and then said carelessly, "Been talking to the guys next door and we all thought you'd like to have this room to yourself."

With his knife in my back, he now laughed in my face. "You won't have to kick me out when you have your readers."

It had been Dad's dream that I should go to Harvard. He had always talked about my becoming "one of those brainy people." I had not given myself much chance of admission, for out of five thousand annual transfer applicants, fewer than forty were accepted. All the signals were against me. I was from Boston, for example, and Harvard sought transfer students from outside Massachusetts. My grades had been good, but Providence was not rated among the top thirty-six universities. And, of course, I was handicapped.

Adjustment problems were more than formidable. At Providence I had lived on a suburban-type campus, but Harvard Square is in the middle of Cambridge, one of the busiest areas of Boston. To reach my classes from the dorm entailed a walk of a mile or more across intersections carrying heavy traffic. (Mobility would be much easier now since they have constructed walkways above the streets.)

I used up an immense amount of time simply getting from my dorm to class. There would usually be some- one around to help, but too often those who came to my assistance did so grudgingly, declaring that they were late for class themselves. Sometimes when I asked for help, the response might be, "Sorry, but I'm going to have to run. Just turn right at the mailbox on that corner and then take a left when you reach the yellow building."

In trying to follow fatuous directions like this I would find myself completely lost. When endeavoring to make up time I often had savage collisions with parked cars, street lamps or other solid objects, which bruised and battered me from head to shin. Facial vision doesn't help when you're in a hurry.

Following a series of head collisions in fast order and with the build-up of concussion over the years, I developed glaucoma, a disease characterized by fluid pressure behind the eyeballs. This pressure caused me intense headaches. On the night of the first heavy snowfall of winter, the pain became so unbearable I was not able to alleviate it with half a dozen aspirins. I had to get to the Harvard infirmary for a stronger anal- gesic.

I felt my way out of the dorm and into the freezing square. The pain was brutal. The snow muffled sound (snow is the blind man's fog) and there was virtually no traffic. I slipped on a sheet of ice and fell. For a while I lay dazed and completely disoriented, the cold intensifying my agony. I was sliding into oblivion when I heard a familiar reedy voice.

"Are you okay? Can I help?"

Ironically it was Cecil who stood over me. He pulled me to my feet and I leaned heavily on his shoulder as he led me to the infirmary. The student who had moved out of my room because he did not want to "mother" me undoubtedly saved my life. Had he not taken that shortcut across the square. I'm certain they would not have found me until next morning.

At the infirmary a doctor gave me a pain-killing shot and I was moved to Massachusetts General Hospital. There an ophtalmologist advised that he would have to remove my eyes at once. To the sighted this prognosis may sound emotionally traumatic, but I barely felt concerned, for my eyes had never been a window on the world. Cosmetically, the ophthalmologist assured me, plastic eyes would be a gain. When I phoned the news to Dad, his only observation was that I should choose a "nice new color."

Although the prosthetic surgery was uncomplicated, I remained in the hospital two weeks, because the doctors were concerned about the possibility of postsurgical infection. Father Bill, now a priest, came down to visit me and read aloud until his throat gave out. Then we talked, he in croaking whispers, of man and church and God. I told Bill frankly how my faith had faltered, failed and flattened out and that in fact I now called myself an agnostic. He was saddened, fearing I would become, as he put it, "an intellectual snob and cynic like so many of those runny-nosed Harvard types."

I warmed to Bill but felt that in my thinking I had now moved away from him. Yet I admired, even envied, his pure faith and childlike acceptance of a personal God who counted human hairs.

This Friar Tuck would always be my cherished friend who, I knew, would never give up hope or his prayers that one day I would fulfill his vision of my becoming a sort of prophet-spokesman for my generation.

In spite of missing two weeks' school, I intensified

my study, for there was little else to do. I planned to
major in psychology. I was greatly assisted in my work
by about eight regular readers, professors' wives who
responded to my appeal for help. The readers read
textbooks to a tape recorder or directly to me in my
room. I made notes in Braille, but relied for the most
part on memory.

Sighted people are often astonished by my memory,
not appreciating that it *has* to be exceptional. An important trick for developing a good memory is to have
a good "forgetary": to be able to discard from the
mind unnecessary trivia. I can carry, for instance,
maybe fifty important telephone numbers in my head
and forget fifty others when I move from one place to
another.

I owe a tremendous amount to the volunteer readers
at Harvard, not only for helping me make the dean's
list in my first year (I was second in my social relations
department) but for helping to fill the vacuum in my
life. The professors' wives often stayed on an extra half
hour or so to discuss current social issues, political
events and the like.

Harvard had a curfew in 1967, and I found a useful
source of income in charging students twenty dollars
each time I'd smuggle in their girls on the pretext that
they were readers.

I was never deliberately ostracized by the students.
It was just that with a handful of exceptions, they
made no attempt to draw me into their circles. Because
I found no real friends in the Lowell House dining
room, I very rarely went there. I would buy one meal a
day, usually at Elsie's Café, and take it to my room,
there to eat alone. I have never felt before or since the
stark, continuous loneliness I experienced in that room.

Loneliness was almost a physical pain, a constant
weight on my heart. Through the thin partition of my
suite I listened to noisy parties given by Cecil, Oliver

and the others—parties to which I was never invited. One Friday afternoon my hopes of ending my solitary confinement were raised. I was on my way back to my room, waiting on a sidewalk for the sound of traffic to quiet before I crossed Harvard Square, when my arm was touched. A young and pleasing feminine voice inquired, "Would you like me to help you across the street?"

I murmured thanks and the young voice reflected, "It must be difficult to get around. Have you ever been hit by a car?"

"Not yet," I replied. "This white cane is just about as effective as a cop's right arm."

We had crossed the street now, and I was suddenly desperate for company. I asked her if she had time for coffee. Her hand left my elbow and I was aware she was looking at her watch. Then she said, "I'm sorry, I've got a studio date—I'm taking ballet. Perhaps later . . ."

I seized the opportunity. "Great. What about dinner tonight? Do you like French cuisine?"

The girl was silent. I tried to picture her. She was small, I realized, and as a ballet student had to be lissome, truly feminine, surely a brunette. I built up an image in my mind.

"Look," I said urgently, "the Sans Souci will send a meal to my room. Oysters, cracked crab or shrimp?"

She laughed easily. "I don't even known your name."

"Tom—Tom Sullivan. I'm at Lowell House—Section R. And yours?"

"Oriana Manarite—Italian, if you didn't guess." Another easy laugh.

"At seven o'clock?"

A pause, then, "That would be nice. Thank you."

When we parted on the pavement I was intensely excited. I phoned the Sans Souci and carefully selected

a menu, finally settling for the chef's recommenda-
tion—coquilles St. Jacques, crème brulée and pink
champagne. The dinner was to be delivered at my
room precisely at seven-thirty. At six o'clock I remembered I didn't have napkins or candles. It took me almost an hour's shopping to find these and half a dozen
roses. I was near panic when I came back to my room
to prepare the table. I stuck the roses in a beer tankard
and whittled down the base of the two candles so that I
could ram them into bourbon bottles. My main concern
was that the plastic plates detracted from the décor.

When Oriana had not turned up by seven-fifteen I
was not in the least put out. Women kept their own
schedules. But when the meal was delivered punctually
at seven-thirty I began to worry about how to keep the
main dish warm and the champagne cold. Ten minutes
later I lit the candles and held the chrome dish of coquilles over the flames until my arms ached.

Nine o'clock, ten, eleven!

Oriana did not turn up at all. I never heard from her
again—no apology, no note.

I did not touch the meal myself, not even the warm
champagne. The sounds of revelry from Cecil and Oliver's party poured salt into my wound. At eleven
o'clock I went out and caught an MTA bus. I suspect
the driver thought I was drunk when I gave him a
dollar and asked for no change. I spent most of that
night traveling on buses or waiting at bus stops. I had
no idea where I was and didn't care. It was dawn when
I returned. I slept until a Sans Souci waiter came to
collect the untouched, candle-blackened dish of coquilles St. Jacques. I don't remember what happened to
the pink champagne, but the sweet and melancholy
scent of roses filled my solitary cell for several days.

My separation from the students stemmed less, perhaps, from my handicap than from the fact that I had
so little in common with the majority of them. Most of

the students had a great deal of money to spend, and most believed, in some cases justifiably, that they were the best scholars in the nation. It was this creed that sometimes produces an intellectual snobbery, a surface cynicism and a collective coldness of heart.

I certainly don't blame Harvard for those unhappiest of days. It is obviously a school that has nurtured some of America's great men. The fault lay in my decision to go there. It was not a place suited to me. I was close to submerging in a bog of despair when two pairs of hands reached out to help me.

The first belonged to a member of the Harvard crew; the second to a paratrooper recently returned from Vietnam.

Leighton Wallingford was the member of the varsity crew, and it was he who suggested that blindness would be no handicap to my participating in a sport he worshiped.

"What the hell," encouraged Leighton. "I usually row with my eyes shut anyway."

"But haven't most of the crew been rowing for years?" I countered. "I mean there has to be some skill. It's not just brute strength."

"You're dead right it isn't. It's masochism. You gotta be crazy or crew or both to run the bleachers at six o'clock on a frosty morning."

The only rowing I had done was with Tom Sly when we had taken a skiff to and from the island off Cape Cod, but because I was a transfer student and not permitted under A.A.U. and N.C.A.A. rules to wrestle competitively at Harvard, I was badly in need of another sport, both to keep myself in shape and to defuse my energies.

It was winter, and the crews were working out in tanks inside a heated building. Initially I was so atrocious with an oar, falling out of my seat and "catching crabs," that I was the comedian at the tank. But with practice and with blisters healed, I made some progress.

What was important about my rowing was that, unlike my wrestling, I did not become a zealot. The sport remained a pastime for me, no more, not a contest in which I had to beat the best.

The more I rowed, the more respect I gained for Leighton Wallingford and the other members of the crew. Oarsmen are a breed apart. There is probably no sport that demands more self-discipline. Crewmen want it tough. Leighton constantly quoted Rusty Callow, the legendary crew coach of the U.S. Naval Academy: "Why is it that some men are quitters and some are not? Why is it that some have the moral and physical courage to go on, regardless of toil and sweat and pain and tears? Rowing beckons such men as these."

Those who have never been in a shell cannot fully understand what the sport does to the minds and hearts of crewmen. Oarsmen have an almost religious feeling for their sport and an extraordinary affinity for one another.

Coach Ed Brown excused me from the punishment of running up and down the stadium bleachers, fearing that I would fall. Every other member of the crew was expected to run fifteen hundred bleachers within ten minutes. This exercise alone gave them legs almost as strong as a mule's and wind to outlast the longest race.

I wished that I had taken up rowing at Perkins. I think that if I had I would have been a good oarsman at Harvard and ready to give up beer and coffee for skimmed milk.

One thing I did have going for me was a natural sense of rhythm and an appreciation of the sport's comradeship, both critical in building up a winning crew. I remember Leighton trying to articulate the team spirit: "It's the only sport in which you can cheat and get away with it," he said. "You reach a point in every race when mind and muscle scream, 'Quit! Quit!' But somewhere a more certain voice of conscience whispers, 'Go on! Go on!' And you do just that. See what I mean when I say we're crazy?"

But for me it was always simply good fun, even when we had to break ice to take the shell out onto the Charles River. Actually I rowed well enough to make the junior varsity second boat for the spring Trident race on the Charles River when we beat both Boston and Brown universities. (But then, Harvard always won!) Later I got to stroke the second boat and I traveled as reserve to Henley-on-Thames in England for the famous international regatta. I didn't make the shell, which was perhaps why Harvard won again!

I would have shed no tears if I had never been selected for a boat, for my enjoyment sprang from a sense of well-being in reaching prime physical condition once again. Anyway, my first experience of a competitive sport in which I had no desire to be a superman gave me a chance to understand what a team really is.

Coach Brown and the other crewmen soon recognized that I would never be a total convert to their sport, never be ready to live monastically in order to conserve energy for the final spurt. So although I found friendship, I was not invited to enter the inner circles. I didn't become one of the "breed apart."

I met Jack Lucas, the former paratrooper, one summer weekend at a bar near home in Milton. I had known Jack slightly as a senior at Providence. I was questioning him about his wartime experiences when he put down his beer tankard and said out of context, "That's something you could do!" (This is a very familiar phrase to blind people.)

"What?" I asked.

"Skydive."

"You've got to be kidding." I laughed.

Another round of drinks stimulated Jack's superlatives about the joys of parachuting. Then I nodded my head.

"Okay, I'll give it a try," I said unsoberly.

As vice president of a skydiving club based at Springfield, Massachussetts, Jack had enough pull to get me into a group of novices. The training the first weekend amounted to no more than learning to jump from a truck traveling over open ground at twenty miles an hour. Wrestling had taught me how to fall and roll, and I fared well enough in this early drill to advance to a controlled parachute jump from a tower about fifty feet high. Three weekends later I was doing static jumps from a low-flying aircraft. The training so far was all so straightforward and safe that I didn't feel any special excitement. I was still in the nursery, still to experience the thrill of a free fall.

In the static jump, the parachute is automatically opened by a tape attached to the aircraft. There is no danger in this jump and little skill required. All I had to do was count so I would know almost to the precise second when I would hit the ground.

"Now," said Jack on the fifth weekend, "are you ready for the big ones?"

I confess to a fluttering in the stomach as I nodded. No blind person had, to my knowledge, ever skydived before. I posed a novel problem and two things had been bothering me—how to know when I was drifting and how to know when the ground was near. Jack and his friends devised a simple talk-down system. They fixed up a small transceiver behind foam rubber inside a football helmet. With radio bands preset, I could receive instructions from both the plane's pilot and ground control. As Jack and I were carried aloft six thousand feet, he repeated instructions on pulling the ring to blossom out the chute and how to tug the stays and "swim into the wind" in the event that I might drift from the safe-landing area.

When finally the pilot turned his head and asked if we were ready, I heard an echo from the past: the Greaton Road gang shouting at me to jump from a high wall into a snowdrift.

Skydivers who have jumped at night will perhaps understand something of what went through my mind as I stood at the plane's door. If there had been a bathroom on the plane I would have paid it an urgent visit. A hurricane wind was howling past my face. The pilot said, "Okay," Jack shouted, "Go!"—and I stepped out in space.

The buffeting and somersaulting in the next few seconds were so marvelously exhilarating that I almost didn't want to pull the cord. But the little radio receiver in my helmet crackled firm commands and so did Jack, who jumped with me and was close enough for me to hear his shout. I pulled the cord and a second later a sudden wrench at my shoulders told me that the chute had trailed and blossomed.

Then I was swaying in lazy arcs that were so sensuously exciting I felt compelled to sing. The motion seemed to slow down time, and as far as I was concerned I might have been drifting toward the moon. But Newton's law of gravity prevailed. My ears popped and then, all too soon, I heard the voice from the tower crackling inside my helmet.

"Okay, Tom," it was saying, "you've got two hundred feet to go . . . one fifty . . . seventy-five . . . thirty . . . Prepare to land." My heels thumped hard; I rolled over, and I was obviously back once more upon my planet earth.

"Wow," I yelled. "Wow, man! Wow!"

What else to say? I have never heard a skydiver adequately describe what goes through the mind on a first jump. It is such a personal, primeval experience, like returning to the sea, that it quite beggars all but the poet's powers of description. Skydiving has been equated by psychologists to a death wish. That's absurd, I think. It is not a thirst for doom but a reaching out for freedom—tangible and almost transcendental—that lures man to this sport. The thrill of the first jump is never quite recaptured by the jumps that follow. Yet I was so excited and elated by my first leap into space that I made thirty-eight jumps before my last and almost fatal one.

Both my skydiving and my rowing were therapeutic for me. They provided escape valves for the critical build-up of frustrations on the Harvard campus. Without these recreations I don't think I could have survived my twenty-first year. But these pastimes did not heal my spirit, being eaten away by the leprosy of cynicism; nor did they answer my urgent need—the need of every human being—for love.

Cynicism and love cannot be companions in one human heart, for they are mortal and eternal enemies.

In recollecting this period of my life, I set out by speaking of disaster. So Harvard proved for me. Yet disaster generally has its boundaries and during even this dreary winter of my discontent there were some moments of comfortable warmth, some sounds of spring, a whiff of fragrance now and then.

Music, which was soon to become the focus of my creative energies, had been virtually in limbo. Latent talent was stirred from hibernation one May evening when I left the dining room at Lowel House (one of my rare visits) and, instead of returning to the loneliness of my room, walked into the lounge. I had been attracted by some lively playing on the Steinway grand. The tune was on the top-ten list—Burt Bacharach's "The Look of Love." I leaned against the piano and began to hum.

The player stopped. "Know the words?" he asked. I nodded and began to sing. This was how the pianist,

Chuck Renner, and I teamed up, though without a hint of where our partnership would lead.

Chuck was a Harvard track athlete, a senior. Our only bond was music and esteem for each other's talents. We would get together in the lounge several evenings a week for an hour or so and soon we attracted applauding audiences. Since I had no plans for the coming summer vacation, I suggested to Chuck that we might try to get paid work at a resort nightclub, perhaps on Cape Cod.

We began to work seriously on a routine, favoring Burt Bacharach, Simon and Garfunkel and black music. We used the student audience in the lounge as a sounding board. If they liked a song it was in; if the applause was thin the song was out. Once satisfied with our routine, I asked Dad for some nightclub introductions. He put us in touch with a Boston agent, who thumbed through a list of resort nightclubs, finally recommending a new one, Deacon's Perch, near Hyannis Port.

"But I gotta keep my name clean," cautioned the agent. "My clients have class. I want you to test out live at Sergio's in Boston."

I don't know how Chuck and I got the impression that Sergio's was an Irish club. Most clubs in Boston were. Anyway, we modified our routine so as to introduce several of the Irish songs that make strong men weep on Saint Patrick's Day. Sergio's was almost full when Chuck and I opened with "The Look of Love." The applause was modest. About ten minutes into our routine, I gave what I thought was a fair rendering of "The Rose of Tralee." One customer in the back of the bar applauded. We followed immediately with our own arrangement of "Danny Boy." This time there was no applause at all, but after about ten seconds a voice as rough as concrete mixer shouted, "Hey, kid, sing 'O Sole Mio.'" As neither Chuck nor I knew the music or the words, we ignored the request and went straight into Bacharach. Still no applause.

When it was time for our first break, the concrete mixer came to the piano. "Hey, kid, didn't ya hear me? I told you to sing 'O Sole Mio.' "

"Don't know it," I protested.

"Learn it," said the concrete mixer. "You don't get no pay if you don't sing 'O Sole Mio.' "

"And who the hell are you?" I snarled.

"I'm Sergio," the voice responded. "I own the joint."

I got the impression that if we didn't sing "O Sole Mio," not only would we not be paid for our entertainment, but we'd probably lose our front teeth.

In the kitchen we buttonholed an Italian waiter (we discovered almost everyone in the club was Italian) and persuaded him to teach us "O Sole Mio." Forty-five minutes later I was almost phonetically perfect and Chuck was able to hit most of the right notes. The applause was deafening. We sang the song three times before the club closed. Sergio was delighted. He paid us $150, twice our contracted fee.

Three days later the Boston agent arranged for us to audition at Tolino's restaurant, Brookline, for the owner of Deacon's Perch. We had gone through about half our routine—which didn't include "O Sole Mio"—when from somewhere out in front a voice drawled, "Okay, you're on my payroll from June fifteenth till Labor Day."

11. Ebb Tide—and the Flow

I had every intention of making this my magic summer. I was twenty-one. I had planned a summer of girls, music, parties, more girls, more parties.

A few days after our successful audition in the Brookline restaurant, Chuck Renner and I headed for Hyannis Port and Deacon's Perch. With my pay check of $150 a week, I envied neither Aristotle Onassis nor Howard Hughes. Chuck and I arrived ahead of the main stream of tourists who pour in from across the country for the Cape Cod season. We set ourselves up in a so-so boardinghouse, occupying a room with two iron beds, two creaking chairs, a carpet with a hole in it and a constant smell of disinfectant. We played at the club six nights a week from nine until two o'clock, and if by the end of the evening we had not separated out two acquiescent girls, we felt we were losing our touch.

Deacon's Perch was fairly typical of the clubs along the Cape Cod coast. It had a restaurant with a menu that featured lobster and New York steak. The long bar, where prices were outrageous, was usually crowded, and half a dozen waitresses in miniskirts were kept busy. The club's décor was vaguely ecclesiastical; the mixed nomadic crowd included a number of free spenders in boat shoes from the yachts anchored in the Sound. And there were always girls, mostly professional hustlers or amateur fun-seekers, who usually arrived in pairs.

At around midnight Chuck and I would take a twenty-minute break from our playing. Exercising his shrewd eye for talent, Chuck would put down his guitar (which he played almost as well as he played the piano.) and report to me that, say, two unaccompanied brunettes had been watching us closely from the bar. This was the signal for us to drift across the room and, in well-rehearsed lines, make our opening gambits.

As most of the unaccompanied girls were expecting to be picked up, and the majority of these were ready for some action, there was not great subtlety in our tactics. Euphemisms were naturally preferred to the earthy Anglo-Saxon name of the game. Our aim was to score every night but we definitely weren't looking for serious involvement.

The question of sexual morality never came up. Were we not part of the new, free-living generation, most of whom had discarded the last restraints and all the shibboleths of puritanism? If there was one unwritten rule, it was that as long as no one got hurt we could do what we liked with whom and whenever we liked; and to avoid hurting anyone we were on guard against any relationship likely to move below the level of physical pleasure. If any girl suggested by whisper or sigh that she was looking for a deeper relationship, she was immediately dropped from the scorecard.

Actually, there was one unlikely character who constantly and irritatingly intruded on my private life. When I unzipped a dress, I heard the ghost of my grandmother telling me she would see me in hell. I could almost see her bony, beckoning forefinger. Grandmother's ghost even managed to squeeze herself into the back of a car and often arrived at a critical moment in the room with the torn carpet!

I was ready to pay for our fun. The first half of the week I lived high, taking my girls to the best restaurants, liberal as an oil sheik in tipping a good waitress twenty dollars. Then, broke by Wednesday, I had to borrow from Chuck or apologize for hamburgers.

By July the Cape was warming up; the parties too. Time meant nothing, for I still had eight weeks before going back to Harvard. My summer was proving to be all I had hoped for. The work was sheer pleasure because I loved entertaining and enormously enjoyed the applause of the Deacon's Perch habitués; and I liked the hustling and even the hamburgers and hangovers.

Then, one midnight at the club, Chuck leaned across and stage-whispered, "Okay, the chicks are here—one brunette, tall, busty, terrific. I'll take the blonde. She's not your size—an absolute honey, but small."

"Have they been here before?" I asked.

"Uh-huh—three nights back. They've been watching us since they came in. The brunette's really turned on."

"Lead me to them," I said.

Chuck had not exaggerated. The brunette introduced herself as Connie Barrenton, a University of Arizona senior. She was confident, witty, her laughter uninhibited. I deliberately dropped a fork and retrieving it allowed my hand surreptitiously to feel the contours of her legs. Connie's legs were beautiful.

The night promised well.

I did not catch the other girl's name at first. Her conversation was overpowered by Connie's aggressive banter. Anyway, the blonde was Chuck's. I wasn't concerned.

My initial setback came when Connie turned down my offer to take her out for a sandwich after the club had closed. I put on the pressure, but she and Patty were on the early roster at the restaurant where they had summer work as waitresses.

So the blonde was Patty. I needed her as an ally.

"Come on, Patty," I protested. "Aren't you hungry?"

She responded quietly and unexpectedly. "Are you really blind?"

"Me blind?" I said mockingly. "How do you think I know you are five foot three, that you've got blond hair and blue eyes, and that you weigh, let's see, a hundred and twelve pounds."

"Hundred and fifteen," said Patty, and she laughed shyly.

I was vaguely aware that Patty was out of place in this setting, that she wasn't a bar girl like so many of the others who drifted around the Cape Cod night spots hunting for laughs, content with the casual relationships offered by young students like Chuck and me.

"Look," I urged, "can't you persuade this mulish friend of yours to share a New York steak with a poor blind musician?"

She hesitated now, not sure whether I was joking. Connie interjected, "Look why don't we meet you on the beach at noon tomorrow. We'll bring the chicken."

Chuck was shuffling his chair. It was time to play our next set. A small, firm hand rested for a brief moment across my wrist. Patty stammered, "I'm sorry, I didn't know . . ."

"Didn't know what?" I asked.

"That you're really blind."

"Nice compliment." I laughed.

"And I—er—love your voice."

"Thank you," I said and, leaning forward, felt a wisp of her hair brush my cheek. I added, " 'S'matter of fact, I like yours too."

Chuck was not able to make the beach for the picnic lunch. His parents had arrived for a visit. Patty and Connie picked me up in a vintage car they affectionately called The Beast. The eighty-dollar Beast had no reverse and no first gear. I was invited to push it to get it started, and then, sweating and breathless, to jump into the moving vehicle.

At this point I could see only one advantage to the picnic. I'd be able to boast back at the club how I had hustled a double.

Actually the afternoon started badly. Patty dropped

the chicken in the sand and when I bit into it, I broke the cap off a front tooth. "Who's going to pay my dentist?" I howled with mock severity.

Then Connie declined to walk down the beach with me. But, still apologizing for the chicken, Patty took my hand. While we ambled along the shore, our conversation was predictably prosaic. She asked me about Harvard and I volunteered that I had spent two years at Providence College.

"Oh, so you're a Catholic?" she inquired.

"Was," I said.

A silence followed until she said, "Then you don't believe in God?"

"Or Santa Claus," I replied.

I stubbed my toe on a rock and swore. Patty apologized.

"Don't worry," I grunted. "My toes are cast iron—they have to be."

The awkward silence was broken by a kid bawling for its mother. Then I said, "So you want to know what I believe? In a nutshell, I would say that religion is for priests and girls in convents."

"I went to a convent," Patty said quietly.

I groaned to myself. Here's raunchy Sullivan with a puritan from Arizona. I covered my irritation with a Harvard intellectual's assault on religion. Oh, sure, there might be some force greater than ourselves. After all, science couldn't explain electricity. If there is a God, however, how can you explain the existence of ghetto slums or a child that's run over by a car or cancer or the murder of innocent people in Vietnam? I stopped short of asking how a blind person could possibly believe in God, but I rambled on, mixing the doctrine of my professors with some Bertrand Russell.

"Naturally every intelligent person is a quester," I added condescendingly. "I'm a quester. That's why I'm at Harvard."

Pretending to slip on a rock, I found an excuse to put my hand around Patty's bare midriff and responded positively to her smooth skin and firm flesh. She wasn't fooled by my fumbling fingers, and with a slight movement she freed herself. The child along the rocks had stopped screaming. The sun was comfortably warm on my back. It was very quiet except for the sea's murmur.

Patty said cautiously, "There are no arguments, Tommy, against what you're saying." Her hand shifted into mine again. "Faith is a very personal thing. You either have it or you don't. You can't debate faith any more than you can debate air, or warmth, or—well—love." Another pause. "Love and faith are very close."

Once again I felt myself respond. It was unprogrammed, non-Harvard, disarming. An awareness of her inner strength touched my mind, sparking a mixture of emotions, alarm among them. It was absurd to be bothered by this childlike girl. Her purity, which I tried to deride, was crystalline, elemental, uncorroded by the acid of cynicism.

Suddenly I was afraid of knowing her. I was as disturbingly aware of her innocence as I was of her femininity. She could destroy my summer, ruin it! All I was looking for was wine and women. This virgin threatened my plans. She might force me to behave, to feel uncomfortable in my dedication to uninhibited hedonism.

I felt I was my father's son, both biologically and physically. Having inherited his genes, I had decided, naturally I carried his lust for living, for liquor and for women. Vaguely and in a way I wasn't able to articulate, this girl walking beside me somehow challenged my convictions.

If at that moment on the beach at Hyannis Port I had had sight, I think I would have left Patty right there on the rocks. I would have run down the sand, gone to a bar, picked up a willing girl and taken her to bed.

But I couldn't run. I was obliged to let her lead me back to where Connie was soaking up the sun.

What at this moment I had never felt and could not possibly measure or imagine was the power of love. Sexual pleasure I understood, and perhaps a lot better than sighted people. But, with the one exception of Hope Francillon in my last year at Perkins, wanting a young woman without the overriding thought of wanting her body—this was totally new. A voice, a whisper, a sense of presence—these now delighted me more than my sense of touch, and deeply mystified me too. But over the next two months I tried through cold calculation and physical separation to fight off the inexplicable, exhilarating and often agonizing power of love that, no matter what I did, seeped into the barred and bolted cell of my heart.

When I thought of Patty, when I wanted her most, when I needed her company and quiet ways, I deliberately sought out other girls—Cindy, Julie, Penny, Greta . . . particularly Greta, whose sexual appetite was never satisfied.

But to try to stop the growing of my love was to try to catch the wind. When Patty was across a room I was conscious of her being there. I was aware of her steps on grass, of her whisper above the cacophony of a barroom.

Desperately I started drinking more. I was laughing louder, chasing after new sensations. I took up water-skiing and became astonishingly proficient. Suicidally, I rode motorcycles, drove cars across a deserted beach (until I hit a jetty wall) and swam foolishly far from shore. One night, to prove to a smashed company that I could outdare the most daring, I jumped thirty feet from the bridge of a moving ferry into the water. I lost my pants and broke my nose. The ferry's crew fished

me from the sea and dumped me naked on the deck. I
dabbed my nose and lapped up the applause.

Patty was often at these parties, ready to dance till
dawn to a calypso band, ready to drive me in The
Beast a hundred miles to a new beach, ready always to
move to my side, to take my hand and weave me
through the tables of a restaurant.

One night, after a particularly wild party that started
when Deacon's Perch had closed and ended with eggs
Benedict under a high sun the next morning, Patty
drove me back to my shambles of a room in the
boardinghouse. I sat down heavily on the iron bed.
Patty turned and walked lightly across the room. I felt
suddenly drained and horribly alone.

"Don't go, Patty," I pleaded. "Please don't go."

She made no reply. My mind was turbulent, my
pulse rising. "Oh, God, Patty, I don't want you to go."

The door handle clicked. For a moment I wasn't
sure if she had left the room or not. Then she
whispered so softly I could barely catch the words.

"I'm still here, Tommy."

Another moment and she was kneeling beside the
bed, holding my head. The very gentleness of her
touch told me that this Catholic virgin who believed in
God and Church's law was ready to love me no matter
what. I felt scarred, brutal, the son of Porky Sullivan.
For the first time in my life I was ready to turn down a
girl's offer of her body.

"Patty, oh, Patty, I'm not your man."

My hands moved to the nape of her neck, under the
cornsilk of her hair. My fingers felt the molding of her
chin, traced the outline of her lips, hovered over her
cheeks. Her cheeks were wet.

I began at last to understand the depth of her feeling
for me. For my sake she was ready to deny her conscience, risk going against her strongest convictions.
Yet she was well aware of my character and reputa-

tion. She knew I might simply add her to the list of my "conquests." Even so, she was ready to make love with me.

I found myself protesting. "For God's sake, Patty, I'm not for you. . . ."

Because I loved this girl of quiet, certain strength and gentle ways, I wanted above all to protect her from being hurt, protect her from being involved with a man who might demand too much of her.

I was sleeping when she left. I didn't hear her go. I dreamed a strange, sad dream. I was in a street with many people laughing, jeering, tugging at my arms and clothes. Dad was there, pulling at me, swearing as I resisted him. On the other side of me I could hear Patty calling out my name. I cried to her, "Fight for me, Patty. If you love me, fight for me." The dream died without resolution of the struggle—or floated, as dreams do, into meaningless sounds and images.

That evening, an hour before I went to Deacon's Perch, Greta arrived at my room—the totally uninhibited Greta, who bounced from mattress to mattress; Greta, who grabbed at sensation as a child grabs at chocolate candy.

I was shaving when she came in, and perhaps the brittleness of her laugh made me aware that she had something on her mind. It could hardly be jealousy, for Greta was notoriously fickle, a permanent threat to every marriage along the Cape Cod coast. I put down the razor and turned to face her.

"What's bugging you?" I asked.

Surprised by my intuition, she sucked in air and then blurted out, "I'm pregnant."

I could not read a face, but I was finely tuned to the inflection of a voice. Hers was filled with sulky accusation.

"Forget your pill?" I said lightly, and at once regretted a remark that released a torrent of accusation and self-pity.

Yes, I, Tom Sullivan, was responsible, she claimed. The girl always had to pay. She planned to go back to college. What was I going to do about it? Her voice started to rise toward hysteria. I found myself thinking of Patty, first of my yearning for her and then of this unexpected opportunity to avoid a commitment to Patty, letting her off too. I interrupted Greta's torrent.

"I'll marry you," I said flatly.

The offer had the effect of a slap in the face. In the ensuing silence I suddenly saw myself repeating the tragic pattern of my father's life. He too had deserted the woman he had first loved—my mother—for the woman who claimed he was the father of her child. I seemed fated to play out the role of my father, a role I hated.

"You're not serious," said Greta.

"I will marry you," I repeated. "At least the child will have a name." I was willing to assume I was responsible for her pregnancy.

The whole scene now seemed like a Victorian melodrama. For the sake of some questionable honor I would leave the girl I loved and marry a body I had enjoyed.

"Well?" I said as I cleaned off my razor. "Don't you want me to make an honest woman of you?"

I had no feeling for her at all—neither pity nor affection nor contempt; just a sense of fatalism and *déjà vu*.

Perhaps she guessed the emotional vacuum in me. Perhaps she began to think—as Patty had not yet thought—of the responsibility of being married to a blind man. Perhaps she had already made up her mind.

Greta said, "I'll let you know—tomorrow." Then she left.

Up to this point I felt as though I had been acting out a costume role. The plot had taken charge. I was reciting lines and the play was moving in its rehearsed direction. But the final curtain refused to fall. After Deacon's Perch had closed that night I went straight back to my room, but not to sleep.

Patty's love swept around the island of my turmoil. I decided it would be better if I didn't see her again. Her opinion of me was less important than her own happiness. Patty was due back at the University of Arizona within a week. She would soon forget me. Someday she would meet and marry a man she deserved. She would meet a man with eyes to see her own.

I reached for the phone and dialed her number. Connie answered. She invited me for an afternoon of water-skiing, but I interrupted to ask for Patty, who came to the phone. She was effervescent and immediately asked when and where we would meet.

"I love you," she said. "I love you. I love you."

I silently bit into my lip.

"Hey!" exclaimed Patty. "You still there, Tommy?"

"Yeah."

"Will you marry me?" she asked and laughed lightly. "I'll wait—till Tuesday!"

"I'm going to marry Greta," I said.

I heard her catch her breath and before the receiver clicked I heard her sob. I cried too. I held on to the phone for almost five minutes, as if it were still some connection to Patty. When eventually I put down the receiver it rang again at once. Assuming it was Patty, I snatched for it. But it was Greta. Her voice was edgy, hard.

"God, you have long conversations," she snapped.

"Sorry."

"I want an abortion," she said.

Abortion is an ugly word, but never uglier to me than when I heard it then. She elaborated. One of her girl friends knew of a doctor. He was expensive. How much was I prepared to pay? She wanted to get it done right away. Finally she threatened suicide if I didn't help.

Agnostic though I claimed to be, my Catholic background had left me with a residue of repulsion against abortion. I suddenly thought of Father Bill. I knew he was vacationing at a hotel twenty minutes down the coast. I managed to get through to him quite easily.

"Bill," I said, "I'm in trouble."

"Are you ever out of it?" he replied.

"I need to talk to you, Bill. It's serious."

"Why do you always come to me at two o'clock in the morning?"

"I thought it was eight o'clock," I replied without humor.

"Your kind of trouble always adds up to two o'clock," said Father Bill.

"Could you meet me for breakfast—at Ed's Café? You know the place?"

Ed's Café was as grimy as they make those ten-table places in resort areas. Across two plates of bacon, eggs and cold toast, I made my first confession in six years. I began by telling Father Bill about Patty, of my love for her and of her love for me. "She's Catholic," I added, "a real one, the kind of Catholic I'd like to have been."

Then I told him about Greta, about the baby, the abortion, the threat of suicide, everything. "I'm not asking for absolution, Bill. You know I don't believe in it. I'm asking what the hell to do."

He asked several questions, reminded me that the Church could not condone abortion and then said, "You'll have to tell Patty, of course. If she's the girl you say she is, she'll forgive you."

"And then?" I asked.

He sighed. I knew he was watching me closely. With a laugh he said, "The Lord has ways of helping even people like Tom Sullivan."

He asked me if I needed money, and when I nodded he pushed some bills into my hands. I later mailed the money—one hundred dollars—to Greta, and I never heard from her again. I heard about her, though. She boasted to a friend that I'd paid for the abortion of a child that wasn't mine.

We left the café and went to Bill's car. I asked him to take me to Patty's place.

Father Bill drove farther than that. He picked up Patty and drove us both to the beach. He left us sitting together on the sand.

Somehow I stumbled through the telling of the story to Patty. I felt her anguish. Sitting there on the warm sand, I understood for the first time what Patty meant when she had spoken of the interweave of faith and love. In her forgiveness, in the reaching out of her arms to me, in the tears we shed together—unaware of anything around us—I saw her love as an incoming tide surging across the scabbed rocks and muddied pools of my life, cleansing and restoring me.

12. Smell of Brimstone, Touch of Bliss

The fuse of our first lovers' quarrel was three thousand miles of telephone wire. Patty and I had been lovers in the richest sense before I had returned to Harvard for my senior year and she to Arizona. Because my scholarship had not been renewed (Dad's income was over the limit and he resentfully refused to help me), I had been obliged to sing at nightclubs to pay for tuition, board and telephone bills—especially telephone bills. Patty and I used the phone at the rate of two hundred dollars a month instead of writing love letters.

At four o'clock on a late-November Sunday morning, I was sleeping in my room with a girl who had driven me home from a nightclub. It was she who answered Patty's call. By the time I reached across for the phone, Patty was still in shock. I could hear her heavy breathing. When she spoke her voice was glacier cold.

"Who is she, Tommy—Greta? Candy? Don't tell me she's one of your readers."

"Patty, I'm sorry. No, she's not anyone you know. I didn't plan it—it just happened."

In a long silence I was aware of the girl going into the bathroom. Then Patty said, "I guess I should be grateful you're not trying to lie."

"I've never lied to you," I said.

Another moment, then, "Tommy, if you still feel the need to have relationships with other girls, I don't need you anymore."

She hung up the phone without saying goodbye.

I at once attempted to justify my resentment. Sure I'd made love to the girl. She wasn't the first girl to share my bed since I'd returned to Harvard. But hell, did Patty really expect me to live like a monk until we met again? Patty knew I loved her; knew that if she were around I wouldn't look at anyone else. Anyway, someone had to drive me to my room from the clubs—and if it was a girl and she offered to stay with me, so what? I wasn't hurting Patty if she didn't know.

The sound of water finding its own level made me aware of the girl in the bathroom. My bitterness and resentment found fresh focus. What the hell right had she to answer my phone! Understandably the girl became abusive when I asked her to leave. She spoke of S.O.B. ingratitude and of where she was going to go at four o'clock on a Sunday morning.

When she left I felt dirty—the kind of feeling I'd had when I masturbated as a kid. My feelings of guilt were not prompted this time by the ghost of Grandmother warning me of the temperature of brimstone. I was deeply conscious of Patty's purity, both of body and of spirit. Thinking of her was like walking out of an over-heated, fetid room into the fresh air of a frosty night. I showered, toweled myself dry and tried to recapture the timbre of Patty's voice, the texture of her skin and hair. Up to now, in my emptiest moments I took comfort from knowing that Patty was within a few hours' flying time, her voice within the seconds that it takes to dial eleven digits on a phone. In hanging up the phone on me, she had seemed to sever the physical connection between us, as if she had withdrawn her hand from mine.

My longing for Patty had accentuated my loneliness at Harvard and lengthened the days. Patty was the only reason why I had stayed on at Harvard. My intention now was to be a practicing psychologist and then to offer Patty the security of my professional work when asking her to marry me.

The reason for graduating had now lost validity for me. Unlike animals, a man must always have thrust and hope. Without aspiration, without a goal, without a reason for tomorrow, a man is already dead or dying. His heart may go on beating, his lungs inhale, his limbs more at the command of the jellied gray matter inside his skull. But effectively, emotionally, spiritually he is no more human than his dog. Death had seemed to crawl into my mind as I put down the phone.

I slept until ten and awakened with the same dead, empty feeling. To sense some emotion again, I felt the need to do something dangerous. I had not skydived in many months. I telephoned Jack Lucas, my paratrooper friend. An hour or so later Jack picked me up and drove me to the Springfield airfield, where the club's duty pilot discouraged us.

"Too risky," he said. "Wind must be gusting at more than twenty knots."

I protested with such vehemence that he changed his mind. "Your funeral," he said—almost prophetically. I buckled on the chute and put on the football helmet with the transceiver in the crown. Maybe because Jack and the pilot were concerned about the wind and I with other things, we forgot to check the transceiver's batteries.

This time I had no sense of fear. I had done it all before. Jack was to be my ground control, and I would jump alone. The aircraft bounced about a bit in turbulence and when we reached 6,700 feet the pilot warned that he was "crabbing" over the landing area. Then he shouted, "Go!"

Once again I was exhilarated during the free fall, spread-eagling my arms and legs and imagining, as does every skydiver, that birds were my kin. I somersaulted twice and swam into the wind, waiting for the command to pull the ring. The only sound was the roaring of the tempest. Something had gone wrong. There wasn't a crackle from the radio in my helmet. I waited five more seconds and then tugged. The parachute jarred my shoulders as it blossomed out.

Still no instructions from Jack Lucas. I was aware now of the gusty wind and had no idea at all of where I might be drifting or how close I was to ground.

I soon understood my peril. A wind of twenty knots could take me a mile or more from the safe-landing area. Jack had spoken of high-tension wires in the vicinity and trees beyond the field. I had no way of knowing whether my body was parallel or perpendicular to the ground. Unless my feet touched first, I would surely break my neck.

There was now no question in my mind that I was going to die. Curiously, I experienced a strange detachment and a sweep of sadness. I did not pray. I did not beg for life. I thought of Patty. I thought of how things might have been. I thought of the last words she had spoken to me—"I don't need you anymore." I recalled in vivid detail our first meeting at Deacon's Perch, our walk across the sand, that early morning hour when she had whispered, "I'm still here, Tommy."

The chute pulled at my shoulders in a heavy gust. Death had to be close. I hoped it would be merciful—quick and painless. Seconds plopped like a dripping bathroom tap, each pause allowing a crystal flash of thought. Do the dying always think of chances lost, of what they might have done, of what they would do if given another opportunity?

If I were given just one more chance I would fly at once to Patty. I would tell her that my infidelities were just palliatives to my utter loneliness, that the women I'd taken to my room were not hustlers, not pickups from the clubs—but in my imagination always her, Patty. She would surely understand, for only Patty had entered the inner chamber of my heart.

Then a crash! It was not the ground I hit, not the sudden bone-crushing impact I'd expected. I'd smashed

into a treetop. I crashed through upper branches, felt a
stab of pain shoot through my shoulder. Stays and
chute tangled and ripped; my body poised a moment,
and then I fell the remaining thirty feet.

I believe that those who have faced what seemed
like certain death—people like racing drivers spinning
to a flaming crash—and who, against the odds, survived, have had the same overpowering thought. It is a
sense of wonder rather than relief, a sense of awe, perhaps. I doubt whether anyone who has felt the rancid
breath of death is ever quite the same again.

I was aware of pain. I had cracked a collarbone and
ribs. When they picked me up they asked me why my
fingernails were bleeding. I remembered then that I
had clawed at frost-hardened soil. I had dug into the
earth to convince myself I lived.

Ten days later, the death I had cheated in a skydive
made its second serious bid. I was now firmly resolved
to fly to Arizona. I had phoned Patty, who was still
cool and full of questions—her own doubts fed by
those of her parents and her brothers, who sought to
protect her from the complications of life with a blind
husband.

The day before I was due to fly, Dad phoned and
asked me to play piano and sing at his club. My fingernails were barely healed, but I agreed. I badly needed
funds. The air ticket had drained my bank balance,
and I wanted to buy Patty an engagement ring. Dad
usually paid the going rates.

I played that night to an almost empty club. At two
o'clock the barman closed the door and left. I went to
Dad's office—the same office, smelling of stale beer
and cigars, where I had been introduced seven years
earlier to Betty and Helen. Dad sat behind his desk,
obviously quite drunk.

I had not seen him in eight months. He sounded old,

crumpled. I knew he was taking pills for a heart condition.

"So you've come for your dough, huh?" he slurred.

"I've come to see you, sir."

"Know how much we took tonight? Ninety bucks. Not enough to pay the rent."

"I don't need to be paid, Dad."

"Can't even pay my own son," he grunted.

"Forget it, Dad. I—"

"Forget it! I'm gonna end it." His melancholy changed to fury.

I heard him pulling out a desk drawer. I thought he might be reaching for a checkbook, perhaps his pills.

"Know what I have here? It's a gun," he bellowed.

Dad had always overdramatized, and I played it cool. I took hold of the conversation and told him about Patty and my love for her and how I hoped to marry her. I was not sure how much he understood until he said, "You're going to mess up your life like me, you son of a bitch. You're going to mess up that girl's life like I messed up your mother's." He pushed back his chair and walked around the desk. Then I felt cold steel at my temple.

"I'm going to kill you, Tommy; then I'm going to kill myself. You hear me, Tommy? I'm going to kill you . . . kill you . . . now."

He was crying, his whole body shaking. The barrel of the gun was pulling at the hair at my temple. Dad could not have realized what he was saying; nor would he know what he was doing if his finger pulled the trigger. If I tried to grab his hand, the gun might easily go off. If I hit him or tried to throw him to the floor, I was sure he would shoot himself, or me, or both of us.

My mind raced, then hovered over the thought of begging him to allow me to say my prayers.

"Dad, let me first make my peace with God," I said quietly.

I knelt on the floor and started to recite the Lord's Prayer. He was above me now, the gun pressing painfully into the top of my head.

" 'Our Father, Who art in heaven, hallowed be Thy name. Thy kingdom come. Thy will be done, on earth as it is in heaven.' "

Dad was swaying on his feet, his knees hitting my chest. I dragged out the familiar phrases.

" 'Give us this day our daily bread. Forgive us our trespasses, as we forgive those who trespass against us.' "

A car horn sounded far away.

" 'Lead us not into temptation, but deliver us from evil. . . .' "

I wasn't thinking of the prayer. I was just overwhelmed by a sense of pity for my father. He had been my hero once. Then I had hated him for what he had done to Mom. Now all I could feel was compassion for his misery.

"Amen," I murmured.

Dad only grunted. The gun was still at my head; his knees still swayed into my chest. I had begun to recite a Hail Mary when Dad lifted the gun and hurled it across the room. I heard the metal crack into the wall and then a soft bounce on the carpet.

He moved around his desk again and sat down heavily in his creaking chair. He began to sob quietly and then hysterically—long shuddering sobs. I stood up and said, "It's going to be all right, Dad. Things are going to be okay."

Now a torrent of self-pity raced out in incoherent sentences. "I can't even pay my son . . . my blind son. Sheila's gonna have another baby. I'm too old. I won't see the bastard grow up. . . . Nobody loves me . . . not your mother, not Sheila, not you, not anybody . . . nobody, nobody."

I leaned across the desk and put my hands on his

stooped shoulders. "I love you, Dad," I said. "Thank you for all you have given me. I love you, Dad."

I walked out of the room, fumbling my way through the tables of the club, and let myself out in the street. I would always be my father's son, but Dad and I had come to a fork in the road and we would now go our separate ways. On the sidewalk, the cold December wind bit into my face.

I took an early flight next day to Tucson, to Patty. Both of us were nervous during our first meeting in four months. There was an awkwardness between us, a probing to find again the mood, the currents that had carried us so buoyantly at Hyannis Port. Our first embrace at the airport was too well rehearsed, unspontaneous, our laughter too easy, our first dialogue skimming over honest doubts and needed explanations.

She was concerned, I knew, about how I would be received by her family. Patty's father, Mr. Steffen, was a man of firm conservative opinion, with the rugged independence of one who has climbed unassisted to hard-earned affluence. He had raised seven children in the Catholic faith.

From the beginning, Patty's mother was warm, outgoing, and I knew at once the source of Patty's femininity and gentleness. But Mr. Steffen made no secret of his caution. He would have to know a great deal more about Tom Sullivan than he could piece together from simple courtesies. It was Patty, not I, who took offense at her father's cold responses to my overtures. Her brothers Bob and Joe assumed neutral ground, but stayed close to my side when I played yard basketball or went riding with them in the foothills.

A few days later I had an opportunity to beard the lion. I found Mr. Steffen alone in his office. We began by talking of football and the stock market, and he expressed surprise that I was knowledgeable both about business trends and about the current form of his favorite Detroit Lions. With some ground gained, and taking advantage of time out to fill our glasses with Kentucky bourbon, I told him that I loved his daughter and that I hoped to marry her quite soon.

He was silent a full minute and then said, "I never asked my wife's father for his daugher's hand. Why do you?"

"I'm not asking for permission," I replied. "We're both adults, and know our minds. I'm asking for what used to be called a father's blessing."

Another silence, a noisy sip of bourbon, then, "Of course, I'm worried by Patty's choice. Haven't I got reason? It's hard enough for a sighted person to make his way in the world. And what of children if you have them? Maybe they'll be born blind. I don't want my daughter to be hurt."

His questions were understandable if foolish, yet I began to like this slow-speaking, solid and successful man, and not only because he loved the girl I loved.

I explained carefully how I had lost my sight—not through genetic aberration but through medical miscalculation. I told him of my scholastic record and of how blindness had reinforced my ambition.

Mr. Steffen heard me out, recharged his glass and then began to speak of Patty as if I were not in the room, as if my blindness made me a sort of nonperson.

"I thought we'd lost her when she was a little girl. Rheumatic fever. Spent most of one night at her bedside—praying. I gave her to God that night. I told God that if she lived I would never control her life. If she wanted to be a nun, that was fine with me. When I took her to the convent school in Beverly Hills and left her at the door, I said, 'God, You gave her to us. She's Yours again.' I sold my Detroit business at a loss because of Patty. We were ready to eat beans and potatoes for this child. The illness left her with a heart murmur. Doctor said to me one day, 'If she was my child I'd take her to the desert.' Six months after we arrived in Arizona she was off medication—looking like an advertisement for oranges. She fell in love with a young New Zealander here at the university. Liked him. Clean, good-looking fellow. Clever too. He was killed in an auto crash just down the road. Patty's faith never wavered. Never will. Too deep-rooted. Now she wants to marry a blind man. No, I'm not going to interfere. If that's God's wish—if that's the sacrifice He asks for giving back her life—so be it. It's gonna be hard. Told her that. I'll abide by what God tells her to do."

My reaction to the soliloquy was mixed. I declined to see myself as a sacrificial penalty, but I respected his sincerity. I resolved too in that moment that I would never do anything to damage Patty's faith.

Not having enough money to buy Patty an engagement ring became an embarrassment when she invited me to give a concert at her sorority house. The sorority tradition was to encircle a decorated candle with an engagement ring, and then to pass the candle around the table. When I arrived at the sorority house, one of Patty's friends asked for the ring. Patty quickly interjected, "Oh, we couldn't find the one we wanted."

I played and sang and kept on thinking about the missing ring and whether Patty's friends were sorry for her, sorry that she was planning to marry not only a blind man but a poor man too. It was such a trivial thing, but the thought was a dead weight in my mind.

At least I could demonstrate that Patty's man had talent. Perhaps it was the pain that helped me put all I knew into my singing and my playing. When I had finished several ballads, I turned about on the piano stool and said earnestly, "You are Patty's dearest friends. I want you to know how much I love her, how much I need her. Although we don't require it for the certificate, I would like to have the permission of all of

you to marry Patty. You have shared part of her life. I
am going to share the rest of it. It would be just great
if I knew—well, if I knew that you approved."

It was one of those rare occasions when I desperately wished for eyes. The girls came up to me, one by
one, to kiss me. My shirt collar was wet with their
tears. No one was thinking any longer about the ceremony of the candle and the ring.

After midnight, when Patty was driving me back to
her home, she stopped at a traffic light and said softly,
"Tom, I believe with all my heart that I'm marrying a
great artist."

Ever since the successful summer at Cape Cod, I
had been thinking intermittently of quitting Harvard
and giving up my plans to be a practicing psychologist.
I had been thinking of becoming a professional musician. Actually the idea had bounced around my mind
from the day when the Perkins maestro had assured
me that I had a good voice and perfect pitch. I knew
too that I could compose. The songs I had sung to the
sorority were mostly my own compositions. But then I
also knew that a musical career is the slipperiest of all
slopes. For every singer, every composer who reaches
the top, a thousand fail.

It was Patty's quiet confidence in my ability that
turned an ardent wish into a firm resolve. Her words
whispered as we waited at a traffic light were not flat-
tery, not starry-eyed adulation; they were pledges of
her future, her life. If I failed, she would have to live
in shacks.

That night we decided on a spring wedding. After
several weeks in Tucson, I returned to Harvard for my
last semester, essentially to fill out time. Ironically, I
now found the work rewarding, for I was assigned to
the staff of a brilliant doctor who was working with
handicapped children. I could have enjoyed psychology
as it is used to help children with special problems,

help them move out of frightening, unnecessary shadows to find real meaning in their lives.

Fresh assurance of my ability to make a career in music was given to me when I received an unsolicited offer to play a Cape Cod nightclub through the summer at a salary of a thousand dollars a week—"enough," I told Patty on the phone, "to support you in the manner in which you are accustomed. Ask your dad if he still thinks I'm a sacrificial penalty." She laughed with delight.

Playing Boston nightclubs six nights a week—among them Brandy's, Lucifer's, Yesterday's and the Playboy Club—I built up bank reserves enough to buy Patty a diamond ring. The day before I planned to leave for Tucson—two weeks before the wedding—I received a phone call from James Robertson, who had been a roommate at Providence. James explained that his brother Tom was giving a party for his business friends and that the entertainer he had engaged for the evening was sick. Would I fill in?

Two hours later Mom was alarmed by a helicopter's landing in our yard at Milton. I had not met Tom Robertson, who had sent the chopper to pick me up, but soon discovered that he was a stockbroker and a millionaire. The guests that night at the hotel were collectively worth several hundred million dollars. When not playing and singing, I mingled with Tom Robertson's friends. At the end of the party Tom called me to the bar. He asked me questions about my future and then said unexpectedly, "How would you like to work for me?"

"As a full-time entertainer?" I laughed. "Was I that good?"

"No," he said. "You can close up your piano, but I'll give you thirty-five thousand dollars a year as a PR man for my corporation."

While my mouth hung wide open, Tom explained

that he liked the way I talked to people and the way his most influential friends seemed to be intrigued by me.

At breakfast next morning I still thought he was kidding until he asked me to cancel my flight to Tucson and fly with him that day to a business appointment in Chicago. Tom owned a Lear jet.

Patty was astonished when I phoned that night from Chicago and more astonished when I phoned the next night from Seattle. I sat in on Tom's business conferences. I heard men talk in millions where others talk in hundreds. Tom promised to get me to the church on time and offered us his Palm Springs home for our honeymoon.

When I eventually arrived in Tuscon, only three days before the wedding, I was four-fifths persuaded that an assured income of thirty-five thousand dollars a year was more attractive than the bottom rung of a musical career.

Once more it was Patty who held me to my course. It may have been at the same traffic light where we had stopped before that she said, "Anyone can wear a business suit and there are thousands who can earn thirty-five thousand dollars a year doing PR work. But only you have the talents of Tommy Sullivan."

The light changed and we moved forward. "Music's a helluva chancy deal," I said.

A moment, and she said very firmly, "I'm ready to be a waitress in any club where you promise to sing." (The time was to come when she would have to make good that promise.)

When Tom Robertson flew in for our wedding, I quoted Patty's exact words to him. He was disappointed, but he gained instant respect for Patty.

Friends and relatives, including Mom and surprisingly Dad, arrived from everywhere. Father Bill flew from Boston to marry us. Since the Saturday ceremony was to take the form of a nuptial Mass, on the Friday afternoon I went to Bill to make confession.

Doubts and fears, like death, are always at our shoulder. We forget their constant companionship most of the time. Then suddenly we hear the rattle of their harness. When I went to see Bill that afternoon, my fears and doubts were riding close. It wasn't for myself I feared, but whether I really could give Patty the life she deserved, the happiness and security I wanted for her.

I asked Bill for a package deal on all my sins but more urgently I asked for an assurance that, in marrying Patty, I was doing the right thing, the best thing for the one human being for whom I would give my life.

I said, "I can't forget that I'm my father's son and that I might want the adventure of other women."

Bill's comfortable voice came through the screen. "I believe you will find that Patty will take from you the best of your nature, your intellect, your outgoingness, even some of your male aggressiveness. And you will take from Patty a portion of her gentleness, her tolerance, perhaps her faith and certainly her love. I believe you will find that in giving to each other you will come to depend upon each other, and this dependence will give you all the protection you need."

It was with a sense of extraordinary elation that I left the confessional box, an elation that peaked at noon next day (despite a momentary bachelor-party tremor) when, in the presence of our relatives and friends, Patty and I exchanged our vows.

The wedding is all scattered, fleeting memories now, but I recall how when Patty was coming down the aisle on her father's arm, my best man, nightclub owner Joe Meldon (Tom Sly was in the Air Force), said into my ear, "My God, she's beautiful, but if you still want to, we can duck out the back door!"

I don't recall much of what Father Bill said, but I do

remember him reflecting, "Some of you may be thinking that this is a marriage of a man without sight to a woman with clear and lovely eyes. I would like you all to think of this wedding as the joining of two people who see life in different ways."

I remember embracing both my parents at the same time, something I had not done since I was a child. Later I told Patty that I had grabbed at "a stupid hope" that my parents might be united once again. Patty typically responded, "No hope is stupid, Tom."

Yet in recollecting the day's montage—Bill's homily, my trembling hands when I put the ring on Patty's finger, the giggling girls scrambling for the bouquet, the toasts and my mother's tears—I resense its lightness as a feather's touch. I could not describe the flowers that filled the church, the color of the bridesmaids' dresses, that sort of thing, but I'd challenge anyone who claims he had a happier wedding day.

I will yield, though, to anyone who boasts he had a more successful honeymoon! We flew to Palm Springs and to Tom Robertson's luxurious pad. "Even the bathroom seems to be carpeted in mink!" exclaimed Patty.

The first night, totally exhausted, we went to sleep before our coffee cups were cold. We spent almost all the next day swimming in or floating on a pool so totally enclosed by a high abode wall that we swam without bathing suits. We weren't aware that the Palm Springs sunshine comes through smog-free skies; and those parts of me not previously exposed to infrared and ultraviolet rays reacted immediately with hot and blistered resentment. I retired to a painful and solitary bed that night.

In certain parts of darkest Africa, I understand, the older women of a tribe are duty-bound to check the consummation of a marriage. If their report is negative, the bridegroom is obliged by stern tradition to return the dowry to his father-in-law. Had Patty and I married in Africa, I'm afraid I would have lost all my cows and goats. For in spite of repeated lubrication with a salve recommended by a pharmacist, those blisters took a full two weeks to heal!

13. Today's Children: Tomorrow's Earth

The honeymoon was over; Patty and I went back to Cape Cod. But our marriage was at once hard-tested.

I was playing and singing at an exclusive nightclub, The Mooring, and now getting my thousand dollars a week. Patty was working as a waitress at the same club and earning good money too. Luxury yachts from Nantucket and Martha's Vineyard lay at anchor in the bay. The Kennedy set were among the clientele: the "beautiful people"—relaxed, witty, wealthy. Most of them wore tailor-made jeans and boat shoes. Night after night the house was packed. The applause was prolonged, stimulating to me. Patty and I had rented a handsome house for the whole season. When the club closed in the small hours of the morning, old friends and new ones came to our home for supper, more singing, drinking. They would stay till dawn. Patty and I made love and slept till noon. In the warm afternoons we often rejoined our new wealthy friends for sailing and water-skiing.

Have I set the stage? Are the sound effects there—the constant clink of glasses, the whine of speedboats? Can you smell cigars, oysters and expensive perfume? Can you hear the laughter, sometimes inane—the deep-throated laughter of a banker, the cultivated laughter of the jet set, the seductive laughter of the hustlers?

Stop the clock at two on a June morning. The club is almost empty. Cars are pulling away from the parking lot. The dishwashers are busy in the kitchen. I am at the bar drinking a last bourbon. Patty is cleaning up the tables. She will come for me soon and drive me home. Some of our friends will already be there. Others will join us later.

There is a woman beside me who has drunk too much champagne. She is giggling and her hands are busy. She leans across me and nibbles at my ear. She rubs a breast against my arm. She is not a hustler; she is probably a divorcee spending alimony. She tells me she is looking for a bed. She knows I am married, knows that Patty, behind us somewhere, is my wife; but this knowledge doesn't inhibit her at all.

I can hear Patty now. She is at the other end of the bar, deliberately banging glasses together. I return the woman's kiss and slide down from the stool. A moment later I am holding Patty's elbow. She takes me to the club's kitchen. From the rigidity of her arm I can tell she's mad. Once behind the swinging doors, she explodes with fury.

What the hell, I tell her. Can I help it if women want to fool around? I've got to socialize. That's my job. That's partly what I'm paid for. That's why Patty is living well. I can't leave. I can't get away from women. "I'm not like you. I can't get up and walk across the room. Most of them bore me, but I'm stuck with them. . . . Good God, Patty, are you really jealous?"

Patty talks to me through her tears. Don't I know what goes through her mind when she sees a woman with a big drunken smile slobbering all over me? Don't I understand that seduction is a two-way thing? And I didn't act all that bored by the farewell kiss either.

Suddenly Patty's control breaks altogether and she leans into me, her head against my shoulder.

After a while she says, "Oh, Tommy, Tommy, I love you. Don't you understand?"

We hold each other close. My body surges with warmth and love for her. She is trembling, crying, laughing. The dishwashers groan and grind. Another waitress bangs through the swinging doors and slams down a tray. We take no notice and embrace.

Then Patty says very quietly, "Tommy, we're going to have a baby."

My mind is jolted. Oh, God, no! Not a baby! I mean we agreed! . . . What the hell? . . . What happened to your calendar? . . . You said it was safe. . . . How do you know? . . .

It was like the first act of a drama. There was tension; literally a life-and-death drama. We have created new life with our love, yet it seems a danger to love itself as our marriage struggles cruelly with the materialism, the pursuit of pleasure, the unexpected, unwanted complication in our lives.

Patty and I had talked sentimentally about having a child someday. We had agreed, though, to wait several years before starting a family. Patty was much more than my mistress and companion, much more than most other wives. She was my eyes. Now I saw her tied down by diapers and feeding schedules, maybe unable, for instance, to drive me to or from a nightclub. I was both resentful and scared of a child who would make demands on Patty's time. As far as I was concerned, this new life in her womb was an intruder, a threat to our life style.

Even the elements began to play a role in our drama. That night when we drove home it began to rain, not a soft Cape Cod summer shower but a driving rain accompanied by rolling thunder. It rained for eighteen consecutive days. The oldest Cape Codders had never known rain like this. They sourly joked about Noah's Ark. Water sloshed in the gutters, emptied the beaches. Even inside, musty moisture dripped off the walls and molded the drapes.

Seeking sunshine, the owners of the luxury yachts pulled up their anchors and sailed south. Hotel proprietors kept their neon "VACANCY" signs permanently flaring. The patrons of The Mooring disappeared. The second chef was fired, the waitresses one by one; then Tom Sullivan, entertainer.

I wasn't really worried. I had taken time out to appear on TV shows, including the Johnny Carson and Mike Douglas shows. Important people knew my name. I would be able to pick and choose my work. But when at last the rain stopped, the clubs either didn't reopen or they could not afford entertainers at my fee.

Patty and I stayed on at Cape Cod until the end of the summer, without work or income. The bills piled up. When the first cold winds of the fall began to blow in from the Atlantic, we found we still had enough money to fly to Arizona. It would be warm down there, and we could stay with Patty's parents, at least until we could get a clearer view of the road ahead.

It was great to feel desert sunshine on our skins again. The skin over Patty's tummy was stretched drum-tight. The memory is vivid of the moment when I first saw our unborn child not as a complication to our lives, not as an unwelcome intrusion, but as our child—not anyone else's, ours alone. We had been sunbathing by the pool of the apartment Patty's father, a real estate broker, had lent us. We returned to our bedroom and were sharing a shower when suddenly Patty took my hands and pressed them to her swollen abdomen.

"Feel it!" she said excitedly.

My hands began to move upward. "There are more attractive areas," I asserted.

"No, here." She laughed and forced my hands against the throb of life within her.

The third party took up the cue and thumped the wall of Patty's stomach.

I carried Patty's warm wet body to the bed.

"Part you, part me," she said softly. "Your bone, my bone; your flesh, my flesh."

"And your eyes," I murmured.

From then until the birth we had a name for our unborn child. We called it "You-Me," and although the baby had no sex, we invested it with all the attributes we relished in each other.

While "You-Me" grew in the warm, safe night of Patty's womb—grew marrow bone, firm limbs and eyes (surely as clear-visioned as Patty's own)—my own career lost momentum.

Some offers came, but I turned them down. Pride forbade me to take on work paying less than what I had earned at The Mooring. Patty's pride took a different form. I was not at first aware just how deeply she resented parental charity. Her father refused to take a penny for the apartment and her mother saw to it that our kitchen cabinets were filled with groceries.

When I rejected a not unreasonable offer from the Tucson Country Club, Patty made her feelings known in a woman's natural way—by silence. One evening tempers flared. Patty's dart hit target when she said, "How much longer are you going to tolerate freeloading?"

I yelled back, "I'm not a flunky who works at any old piano bar. If I take this job I'll be sliding down the slope. God knows it's been hard enough to get to where I am."

"Where you are," said Patty, "is living off my parents."

It was a stinging back-and-forth until our quarrel ended as our quarrels had always done, in tears and tender touches and the knowledge that below the surface storm there lay strong and certain currents of our love.

The next day I made an appointment to see an agent with contacts (so he claimed) in Las Vegas. There are some good agents, men of energy and intuition who earn their 10 percent. There are also bad ones, who are the pimps and parasites of art and artists. The hand I shook that day was pudgy, clammy, cold; the voice oily, patronizing. I was aware that when he was talking to me he was looking at Patty. He spoke mendaciously, I'm certain, of having played some part in Barbra Streisand's career, and he dropped other names of stars like lumps of lard. In short, asthmatic sentences, he lectured us on dedication to the entertainment industry, and then, turning to Patty, he inquired, "Are you ready, Mrs. Sullivan, to sacrifice your marriage for your man?"

"I don't understand," said Patty.

I could almost see the agent's tongue wetting his upper lip. "How frank should I be?" he oozed. "Sex is the quick way to success. There's a male casting coach, eh, Tommy? You know what I mean. There are women behind the men in the executive suites. Tommy won't have trouble."

He laughed and his laughter was uglier than his words.

Patty was already rising from her chair when the 10-percenter added, "If you want to win, Mrs. Sullivan, you'll have to pay the price."

Until this experience, Patty had never retreated from her convictions that I could and would achieve success in music. Now she wavered and her wavering coincided with pressure from an unexpected quarter. To fill in time, I had started to coach wrestling at Tucson's Catalina High School. The school had hardly won a wrestling match in years. Now they were winning every match. I was not taking any fee for coaching a sport I enjoyed, and there was not much that could please me more than helping forty enthusiastic kids. Advised by Mr. Steffen of my Harvard background in psychology and English, the chairman of the school board approached me with an attractive offer to become a full-time member of the faculty. I would be encouraged to start a music department and to undertake student counseling.

Patty and I talked about the offer very earnestly. We were in bed and against my thigh I could feel the energetic kicks of our unborn baby. Both of us were thinking of the future of "You-Me."

Here, in a Tucson suburb, we could find a home, the security of a job in education. Here we could avoid the struggle, the uncertainty, the greasy 10-percenters of a musical career. Here we could live if not the exhilarating life I had hoped for, then at least a comfortable life and perhaps one that counted for something too.

We eventually decided to postpone our decision. Then fate kicked our lives around a critical corner. I met three young musicians, two guitarists and a drummer, who asked me to form a group with them. Technically the three men were no better than advanced amateurs, but I was impressed by their understanding of the contemporary sound. Up to this point both in my own compositions and in my songs of preference, I was a balladeer, and I had recognized the need to include rock music in my repertoire.

I was always searching for an individual style, some form of music that would make me unique. These young Arizona men gave me a chance to explore a new area of music so that I was able to vary my routine not only from Bach to Bacharach but from soul to hard rock. Using the group, I was able to come to terms with my own strengths and weaknesses. For the first time, too, I was obliged to convey my musical ideas to sighted musicians. I devised a system of dictating melody lines and chords on tape, measure by measure, which the group would then copy onto sheet music. It was in this period that I started the practice of keeping a cassette recorder at my bedside because most of my ideas came to me at night. My main problem in leading the group was that I could not read a master score. I was obliged to memorize all the parts. But this constant strain on memory greatly expanded my musical comprehension. I soon found myself able to filter out the sounds of the different instruments. This enforced ability to break down the different sounds led me to writing arrangements and orchestrations without a piano.

Building up the group to a professional level of competence was demanding but exhilarating work. Although we were no threat to the Beatles or the Rolling Stones, we worked out a routine that earned us a Tucson nightclub contract. Although the pay was modest, the pull of a full-time career in music became compelling once again. The day we received an offer of a three-week engagement in Los Angeles was the day I turned away from the security of a career in education.

Had Patty and I been able to see the rock-strewn, bruising road ahead, I wonder whether we would not then have elected for the Catalina High School campus and the purchase of an air-conditioned adobe house on San Annetta Road.

On Good Friday, before I left Tucson for Los Angeles, "You-Me" was born. (What more auspicious day for the advent of a "saint" and the fulfillment of grandparental hopes!)

In the weeks before, Patty and I had studied natural childbirth and found a doctor who agreed to allow me to be with Patty in the delivery room. The fragment of human life we had almost rejected at conception had long since drawn us into the full adventure of birth. The time lapses between Patty's contractions were shortening dramatically when we scrambled into Saint Joseph's Hospital. There I helped her with her breathing, massaged her back and held her hands when the pain seized her body. "You-Me" was not to be hurried into the world of light.

Patty was calm and full of courage; not so her mother. Although Mrs. Steffen had given birth to seven children, she was now a wreck. She came up from the hospital chapel holding a bottle of holy water, believing that a sprinkling on Patty's forehead would ease the pain. But in her agitation she poured the entire contents down Patty's back. Patty let out a scream of protest that echoed down the corridors. Mrs. Steffen fled. Patty was wheeled into the delivery room, and as if to discover what the uproar was all about, "You-Me" heaved head and shoulders into view. Moments later I heard my daughter's cry.

While the baby was still slippery as an eel, the doctor let me hold her, feel her limbs, her water-wrinkled hands, her damp hair and blinking eyes—eyes that, as they cleared and focused, would provide another window on my world.

Then we kissed, Patty and I, very gently, and we wept together in our joy. We were both twenty-three years old, and life seemed to be marvelously good to us.

That evening, still overwhelmed by a sense of wonder, I contemplated the future of my daughter— not only her dreams and desires, but the world she would find as she pushed forward toward the discovery of her own personality. These thoughts crystallized into a song I called "Today's Children: Tomorrow's Earth." Patty was deeply moved when I sang this song to her a few days later. It must have been then that I finally recognized my best faculty to communicate ideas and feelings was through music.

We named the baby Blythe and brought her home. She seemed as fragile as porcelain, and at first I was very frightened of holding her. She was about ten days old when I nearly drowned her. Patty was bathing

Blythe in a plastic tub and asked me to hold her for a moment while she left the room to find some powder or something. When Patty returned a couple of minutes later, she shrieked with horror. Unwittingly I had allowed Blythe's head to submerge and she was apparently blowing soap bubbles. Blythe seemed none the worse for gargling bath water, but it was a long time before Patty again trusted me with baby care.

Blythe was a good baby of irresistible charm. So now we were three. It was at this time that we made another addition to the family.

If the universe has design, then the hundred billion cells that make up fang, fur and tail of a German shepherd named Heidi were made and multiplied for me. We found her, one of a litter of eight, in kennels owned by friends. From the day when she first tugged at the nipples of the bitch who bore her, Heidi was a maverick, unique, selfless, always ready to protect the runt of the litter.

Only one puppy in a hundred is selected for training as a Seeing Eye dog. No sooner had the trainer spotted Heidi than he nodded his head. The other dogs, the rejects, were returned to a life of ease, to a ten- or twelve-year span of guarding homes, romping in back yards or barking at the mailman. But just as a monk elects for hair shirts, celibacy and cloisters, Heidi seemed to ask for the stern discipline and self-denial of the trainer's camp.

I cannot describe Heidi's form and markings. I know she is tall, slim-flanked, deep-chested, and that she can hold an egg uncracked in teeth that can crush a baseball bat; that she knows how to toss a ball into my lap instead of at my feet. Heidi loves to play, loves to run on a beach and chase a cat over a fence or up a tree. Yet Heidi is at her proudest when she wears the guide dog's harness on her back, when she becomes my eyes and leads me across a busy thoroughfare—or, for that matter, to a restaurant's restroom or to the proper counter at an airport. With Heidi at my side I am ready to travel continents—and do.

The next two years are etched in my memory as only yesterday. I no longer must strain for names and places, for sounds, smells and touches. The peaks of petty triumphs, the troughs of fear, the hopes and disappointments are all still vivid to me. How strange it is that the happiest moments during these times seem to have been the simplest ones, the moments when we were stripped of all but faith and love.

Patty, Blythe and I walked the precipice's edge—especially during the time when we were back in Boston. There we lived in a basement apartment, lit only briefly each day by sunlight coming through the wheels of cars parked against the sidewalk curb. Professional pride had long since vanished. I would take any work, even if it brought in only twenty dollars toward board and rent.

I held one such job for several weeks. We had sold our luxury car and bought a battered Volkswagen. The nightclub was forty-five minutes' drive away. Early each evening Patty would place Blythe in the back seat and drive me to the club. She would then return and put Blythe to bed. At one in the morning Patty would set out again with Blythe and pick me up and drive us back to our basement home. Each evening, come snow or fog, Patty spent three hours on the road. When we had deducted the price of gas, our night's profit might be fifteen dollars.

And the next day, while I baby-sat Blythe, Patty scouted about to find the cheapest markets. Others have lived on thinner fare, I'm sure, but it was a grim time for us.

Actually there was only one day when we were absolutely broke. The coins in Blythe's piggy banks were barely enough to buy us a macaroni supper. Patty had taken a part-time job as a waitress. She had gone to work that morning only to learn that she had been laid off. When she came home and told me, I was as close to despair as I have ever been. I had almost persuaded myself that I was a total failure, I told her.

"Get me a tin mug and I'll stand at the street corner," I grunted.

She laughed. "I'm going to read you something I found in a women's room about a month ago."

"Do women write on lavatory walls too?"

"It's a poem,'" said Patty. "I guess somebody dropped it."

"Not a list of telephone numbers?"

She ruffled about in a shoe box until she discovered the piece of paper. "Here it is," she said. "It's simply titled 'Fear.' "

(We still have the crumpled sheet of paper in a file of memorabilia. As the poem was unsigned, we have no way of crediting the poet.)

Patty read aloud in a firm, melodious voice:

"Fear is a liar, poisoning today
  With fantasies of what may come tomorrow,
  Until each joy is shadowed by a sorrow,
  And dreading it, we leak our lives away.
  If we have wife and child, we fear to part;
  And if we long, we fear we won't attain,
  And snatching at it—even as we gain—
  Forfeit the heaven, the harmony, the heart.
  Fear is a liar. Truth is what God molds
  Our days in love, and with the same precision
  As he makes a wing for flight, or petal fold
  Within a sheath, or shapes an eye for vision
  He hands us strength to welcome what is right,
  Then, swift and sudden, hurls us our delight."

I took as much comfort from Patty's faith as from the rhymed, inspiring lines. I asked her to read them to me again. We talked for a while about the lies of fear. We began to find our dreams once more—slowly, but we found them.

But the immediate problem that night was supper. "Your mom's a great cook," Patty suggested.

"Who was it," I countered, "that once accused me of freeloading off her parents?"

"We're all even," said Patty. She laughed, but we were desperate.

When we bundled into the Volkswagen, Patty did not notice that the gas gauge was at empty. Halfway to Mom's house, we had reason to bless the engineer who had conceived the idea of a reserve tank. The journey out to Milton was a cliff-hanger. The VW engine coughed for the last time a hundred yards from Mom's driveway.

We actually stayed with Mom for several weeks while Patty and I hunted for work. We would have remained longer if my mother had not kept referring to me as "that bum who is going to finish up exactly like his father." I couldn't have cared less what Mom called me. Hunger dulls insults. But Patty was infuriated and did not understand that Mom was really trying to goad me into taking what she called "a proper job." As far as Mom was concerned, being a nightclub entertainer was a step toward lechery and alcoholism.

Patty and I found occasional work, so I never had to resort to the tin mug. When precarious financial independence allowed our return to the basement apartment, we could not have been happier in the west wing of a palace. We not only survived, we even saved enough to allow Patty to take a night coach to Tucson to help celebrate her father's sixty-fifth birthday. If her sisters noticed that she was wearing the same dress she had worn a year before, no one was tactless enough to mention it. What they did not know was that Patty had made one can of hair spray and one jar of face cream last six months to help her buy Mr. Steffen a birthday bottle of his favorite bourbon.

All these memories are not wrapped up in melancholy, however. Far from it! They glow with warmth. Nights when I had no work, our friends, Tom Sly and his new wife among them, and Billy Hannon and his girl friend, came to see us. Basement laughter rocked the building and Patty always found more potatoes for the Irish stew. Tom brought beer, Billy steaks and for fascinating hours we played the game of Jeopardy.

One evening when the thermometer was ten degrees below, Tom Sly could not start his vintage car to go home and called me to help out. We pushed and heaved and slithered on the ice until the engine caught. Tom puttered on his way, quite forgetting that he had left me stranded in the street. I was wearing pajamas and a robe and by the time I found the railing and the basement steps, my teeth were rattling like castanets. It was Patty who thawed me out, using the most primitive and most satisfying of methods. So when Patty became pregnant once again, we could honestly hold my closet friend responsible!

But these two years were not all basement living, heaped blankets, tuna sandwiches and untuned barroom pianos. We had another marvelous summer at the Cape, where we rented a clapboard beach cottage—an artist's dream. With careful budgeting of good pay we built up our reserves again. By the time our son, Tom Sullivan III, was born, we had enough to start planning the home I had promised Patty on our wedding day.

Serendipity is a word that trips so lightly off the tongue that we fail to mark its weight. Few know the tale of the Three Princes of Serendip, who, when traveling far in search of fortune, discovered by chance far richer treasures along the way. Without going too deeply into the philosophy woven around Horace Walpole's fable of the Eastern travelers, let me say that we were diverted from our trail and discovered by chance and "along the way" that the home we dreamed of was not to be among the dunes and grasses of the Atlantic coast but on a sun-splashed cliff in California.

In our first hungry years of marriage, I sometimes still had doubts about making a career of music. I remembered that Harvard had qualified me to set up as a psychologist or a school counselor and that Tom Robertson's offer to take me into his stockbrokerage remained firm. But maybe because Patty didn't lose faith in my musical talent, particularly as a composer, I never totally lost sight of my goal of achieving recognition as an artist, and I never let pass any opportunity to broaden my musical experience.

For instance, while we lived in Boston I often visited the famous Pioneer Club, an old building at the end of an alley that was frequented by many great black artists, including Count Basie, Ella Fitzgerald and Duke Ellington. I was the only white musician encouraged to perform at the Pioneer Club, presumably because the black musicians knew I was truly color blind. Incredible soul and jazz sessions lasted from two o'clock until dawn. Over chicken, grits and potato salad, I listened for fascinating hours to stories of struggle and success. Many black musicians had experienced racial persecution from bigoted Southerners. Some of the musicians were bitterly anti-white, but they laughed when I told them I didn't choose the color of my skin.

"Okay, whitey, sing your song," someone would shout across the room, and when I sang soul or spirituals they loved me.

In the Pioneer Club I got to know the drug scene. Many of the musicians, including some of the good ones, quite genuinely believed that the only way they could get into music and separate themselves from distractions, particularly from their audiences, was through drugs. I could never understand this attitude because I felt the need to communicate through singing. I couldn't see people but I still wanted to know audience reaction and not be screened from people by dope. Actually, I found I was at my best when I was tensed and totally aware of the critical attention of people out front.

Also while we were living in Boston, I made my first album and began to write a rock musical. The album bombed, not because it was without some merit but because we didn't have the money to promote it and because, shortly after it was released, the record company went bankrupt. It was one of those occasions when I remembered President Johnson's advice to me—no experience is a bad one unless we fail to learn from it.

The musical, *City Huck 'n' Tom,* was about two boys seeking adventure, not on a Mississippi raft but in the bustling streets of a great metropolis. One boy was an optimist, recognizing virtue in everyone he met, including pimps, prostitutes and drug peddlers. The other boy was a cynical realist, convinced his survival depended on his cunning.

While at work on the musical, I realized I was really writing about myself—about the one Tom Sullivan who believed that life had some meaning and that there was good in the worst of us; and about the other Tom Sullivan, who was constantly drawn to cynicism.

Some people connected with show business suggested that *Huck 'n' Tom* might be made into a film. This prospect led Patty and me to a decision to go to Los Angeles, the capital of the entertainment world.

On Hollywood and Sunset boulevards there are walnut-paneled offices where artists' contracts are signed—contracts that decide what music will be heard over car radios, on campuses, in clubs and concert halls throughout the Western world. These offices are as closely guarded as dictators' palaces, but in my friend Tom Robertson I had a powerful ally and one who had hardly less conviction of my talent and potential than Patty herself. Tom first took me to the inner sanctums. The outcome of these meetings is still not settled, but what can be said is that, at the age of twenty-six, I have reached a point of heart-stopping expectations in my musical career.

Yet as exciting as anything that happened in the board rooms of the music corporations was the day Patty drove the four of us and Heidi to see friends who live in a wooded community on the coast, not thirty miles from Hollywood and Vine. Below the cliff the Pacific surf swept up a sandy stretch of beach. The air was soft-scented with the smell of lemon trees and eucalyptus. We walked a sun-warmed path and heard the cries of gulls, the sounds of tennis rackets, horses' hoofs and children's laughter. It was Sunday, and a church bell was ringing. Beyond the church there was a house, white-walled, with a fluted red-tiled roof (so Patty told me), Mexican in style. Our friends noticed a "For Sale" sign staked into the lawn.

Suddenly we knew, Patty and I, instinctively that this was the place, this the house, this our home. Here we would raise Blythe and Tommy. Here I would compose and write. From here Heidi would take me safely to the surf and sand.

I swam that day. I swam with Heidi through the surf, far out into deep water. There I sang for joy. The world was surely mine.

14. Reaction and Reality

I was asleep the morning when Patty took an early call from the Braille Institute. She told me about it later when I came out to the kitchen for breakfast. She spoke casually, too casually.

"By the way, Tommy, the Braille Institute phoned."

"Well?"

"A Miss Mildred somebody—I've got it written down."

"What do they want?"

Patty filled my coffee cup. "They want you to speak."

"To the staff?"

"To the blind people."

"And you told them no."

"I told them I thought you'd love to do that."

Anger spurted like a cut artery. "What the hell? What right have you to tell anyone that?"

Patty was cool, quiet. "Don't you sometimes feel obligated, don't you—"

"That's not the point," I stormed. "What right have you got to say that I'll be a spokesman for the blind?"

"To the blind," corrected Patty. "Call and cancel if you want to."

"You call them. You got me into this thing. You can get me out. Give Miss what's-her-name any excuses you like. Just tell her I won't do it."

"Tommy, you've got so much to give. You—"

"Then send them a donation."

Patty flipped the toaster switch. "Anyone can give money, Tommy. You can give hope. You can give—inspiration."

"No one gave me any. I made it on my own."

"People helped you make it."

"Not blind people. My God, Patty, if I'd let some people have their way I'd be tuning pianos or weaving baskets."

Patty buttered the toast and put it on my plate. For a moment we ate in silence, then Patty said, "If handicapped people could only see you, Tommy; if they could only hear you. I mean, if I talked to blind people they'd say, 'What do you know? How can you understand our problems?' But you . . ."

"If they can't make a stand on their own, I can't help them. Nobody can. Can't you see I've spent most of my life fighting to get out of the pit, fighting to get away from blind people? Blind people make me uncomfortable, depressed."

Patty sipped her coffee; then she talked over her cup. "You sound as if you're afraid, Tommy. I can't think why you should be. You are strong. You've got a magnetic personality. You influence people. Even animals are drawn to you. Nobody can hurt you."

"Why the hell should I be scared? It's just that at this point in my life I'm fighting to succeed in the most competitive business in the world. I can't afford the gloom these blind people would give me."

Patty was still controlled. I wanted her to shout at me. She said quietly, "We have human obligations to each other. There are so many people in your past— Tom Sly, your dad—who gave you so much time and help and love."

"Okay, maybe by your standards I'm wrong. Maybe I'm just a selfish bastard. But at least I'm being honest. I don't want to do this. We've got enough problems without creating new ones. We're living pretty well because we're living in a sighted community. I'm out there killing myself in a mainstream for you."

Patty came to my shoulder and refilled my coffee cup. "I'm not asking you to go back to blind people on a full-time basis. Just every now and then—just to touch their world. If they could only see your zest for life, if they could see what you've done . . . There are hundreds of Tommy Sullivans out there waiting, needing to be convinced that they can—make it."

I was too close to losing the argument and was determined to end it. I called Heidi and strapped the harness on her back. "I'm going out," I said. "I'm going to the beach."

I did not know at the time that Patty followed me to the cliff edge. She watched as Heidi led me down the path to the surf. If the next scene were on film we could split the screen here. In one shot I would be seen against the water, tripping occasionally on bundles of seaweed. In the other shot Patty would be seen silhouetted high above me on the cliff edge. The sea gulls would be weaving and crying above our heads. If I were to compose music for such a scene, I would include the sound of waves, the cry of gulls, try to get across the mood of our physical separation and the abrasive contact of our minds and spirits.

And in film we would probably hear Patty's thoughts spoken as a "voice over," in the screen writer's jargon. We would understand her distress and her longing for me to be the man she felt convinced I could be. She knew me as a man who pursued life, his days, passionately, even violently, a man who refused to look back, refused to be thrown by disappointments. But deeper than her hope for my material success was her longing for me to help other handicapped people, those who found the struggle beyond their strength.

Later Patty told me the thoughts that had come to her. She had thought: I know how hard it's been for you, Tommy, to climb out of the blind world. But I have seen you with people in need—with the neurotics, the depressed, the jealous, the poor, the suicidal. I have seen you give them hope, infect them with your own enthusiasm. But please, you mustn't reach out to anyone because of anything I want for you, because of anything I said, or even because you know it's the right thing to do. Go to people because you're strong; I know how much you do care. I love you, Tommy, because you are what you are, but let me help you become what you can become.

Down on the beach Heidi was tugging at my arm. She was proud of being a working dog, resisting the temptation to chase and scatter the gulls and sandpipers. She stopped at a ridge of rocks and then led me carefully over them.

I was thinking now of Patty, of the home she had given me, of the thousand meals she had cooked and served, of the warmth of her body, the silk of her hair, of Blythe and the baby son she had borne. I desired in this moment, desired with climactic urgency, to see her. I knew that other men admired her, envied me her beauty, her femininity. Because of my blindness, our marriage was more honest, open and free than any other marriage that I knew about. Yet I knew our relationship might be damaged, even threatened, by our breakfast quarrel. If Patty tried to make me do things I did not want to do, if she put pressure on me, if she curbed my independence of thought and action, the tightly drawn, fragile bonds of total intimacy could snap or, worse, harden into steel.

I thought how in a perfect relationship between a man and a woman neither should feel the chafe of bonds.

The surge and roar of surf clears the debris of the mind, crystallizes thought. Perhaps this is because the sea is so obviously eternal, and against its limitless stretch of time the problems, the issues of the moment are recognized for the trivia that they are. The sighted can find perspective by scanning the night sky, can philosophize by searching the embers of a fire. But for me sound is always the main catalyst to thought—the sound of raindrops on a roof or wind stirring leaves or a distant locomotive in the night. And a prime catalyst is the sound of the sea.

I had walked a mile, perhaps, with Heidi at my side, when I began to think of the talk I would give if I were to accept the Braille Institute's invitation and speak to the blind people there, many of them completely lost in their dark world—self-pitying, miserable. I would insist on talking to the administrators too. I would tell them of my childhood and pay tribute where it was due to the dedicated people who had helped me. Mostly I would talk in anger.

I thought of how a child goes to a blind school like Perkins carrying with him no sense of personal identity, having had little or no contact with other children. "Pity! Pity!" I almost spat the word into the sand. If the blind child was a girl she would hear over and again the phrase, "Oh! Isn't she pretty, but what a pity she's blind"—words whispered behind a hand, spoken behind a nursery door.

I reflected on how a blind child is caught, trapped in the web of "blindisms," how he is surrounded by other children with his own handicap and with children who have other problems such as mental deficiency, which not infrequently goes with blindness. I recalled with bitterness the regimentation at Perkins and how, when I struggled to find my own identity, I was seen as a disruptive influence because I refused to be contained by the system.

It was upon the administrators that my anger focused, upon self-satisfied men like Dr. Solomon Wise, so convinced that they were doing a great job because they provided good equipment and a beautiful campus. Hadn't Dr. Wise signed a check for a million dollars to build a huge bomb shelter stacked with rations and oxygen cylinders? The steel and concrete would be there a million years from now; the rations too, maybe. How much could have been given to so many students had that million dollars been spent on extra teachers, on individual care!

With only gulls, sandpipers and Heidi to hear me, I made a sort of speech as I walked down the beach. I spoke of the two types of teachers who instruct the blind—those who remain at school for about a thousand years, whose voices crack and tremble with age and boredom; and the young teachers, idealistic, highly trained, compassionate teachers like Hope Francillon and Joan Baez, who, after two years or so, give up their jobs because of their frustrations. Of course, there are exceptions in both groups.

I thought of the desperate need to integrate blind children into the sighted world, the competitive, exciting, challenging real world outside the walls. The reason blind children often retreat into their private frightening or (as tragic) comfortable world is that the schools fail in their first task, which is to show them life as it truly is.

Imagining an audience of administrators in front of me, I said: "Try to get inside the mind of a child surrounded by other blind kids. He is already anesthetized to the real world. Unless he has a mother like mine, he looks like a slob because nobody has told him how to label his clothes. No one has taught him that a light-blue jacket, a white shirt and gray pants go well together. He has already begun to shake his head back and forth as if he were watching a Ping-Pong game. He is already picking at his eyes and his movements are becoming spastic. He doesn't even know how to write his name. No wonder when he becomes an adult he is ready to run back to the security of a blind institution. But who's responsible? Who was it told him that the only jobs he could do effectively were caning chair seats and plugging in telephones?

"You want to help a blind child? Then start by teaching him the common courtesies: how, for instance, to turn his face toward the person who is addressing him, how to dress well, to brush his hair, how to mix with sighted children, not as a freak, not as someone to be pitied, but as a person, an individual with feelings and hopes, little hells and talents too.

"It's integration into, not separation from, society that the blind child requires. Integration isn't satisfied by occasionally bringing a few busloads of sighted kids onto a campus like Perkins. I remember hearing a visiting sighted girl at Perkins dance saying to a sighted boy, 'Gee, we could have gone to the drive-in tonight, but think how good you feel by allowing these blind kids to walk all over your feet.'

"Genuine integration is effected in a simple, natural way—by introducing, say, two or three blind children into a church club or boy or girl scout group. Then neither the sighted nor the blind children are conscious of a charity deal."

In my speech addressed to a nonexistent audience of administrators of blind institutions and to teachers, I spoke of the critical importance of communication with the parents of blind children; of how parents could be led to understand that they were not to be pitied but rather challenged to excel in parenthood. I referred to the need for job orientation and the fullest assessment of a blind child's skills. Obviously there were many jobs beyond the capability of the blind person—he could not, for instance, be a baseball umpire or a surgeon!

Yet there were a hundred jobs for the blind, jobs ranging from the practice of law to computer operation, from counseling to photo darkroom work—jobs to exploit the manual dexterity and intellectual skills of men and women who do not have sight.

Then I spoke to my nonexistent audience of the

blind themselves. "For God's sake and your own," I exclaimed, "don't throw away your time on self-pity. Only you will suffer if you're sorry for yourselves. Depression just wastes time. Make use of your handicap so long as you don't inflict physical, mental or spiritual damage on others. Your handicap can be your best asset for gaining exactly what you want. People are already well disposed toward you when you first meet them.

"When I attend a business meeting and have my Seeing Eye dog beside me, the people at the meeting are ready to give me almost anything I want—at least in the first five minutes.

"The handicapped person has to become the ultimate realist to know his skills and his potentials. If he fails, the community will say, 'Oh, that's just another handicapped person screwing it up. Isn't it too bad.' Those words, 'too bad,' are the most malicious and callous words ever uttered, even when spoken with love. We blind, we handicapped, have an inconvenience, often a great inconvenience, but this inconvenience doesn't have to be a weakness. It can be our strength and, paradoxically, it can give strength to others.

"It is not the world that has to adjust to us. It is we who have to adjust to the world. We are live, viable creatures. We are people. There is not one of us who cannot do some job and do it well. The hard task is to begin, but once you've made a start, keep going and your world will suddenly expand in excitement and challenge. You will astound and delight your families. You will elate yourselves. And once you have learned to walk, you can begin to run. . . ."

My speech drew no applause. The only sounds came from the surf and sea birds. Yet I felt absurdly exhilarated, as though I had got home my points, as if there were people out there—wretched, self-centered people—and I had helped them make some bid for life.

From early childhood I had always been ready to run, sometimes too fast, recklessly. That was when I'd been hurt. I had had to understand that there were limits to my speed; there were hurdles too high for my leaping. My running had to be controlled, held within my strength and capability.

Now I tugged at Heidi's harness and turned about on the beach. I began to run back toward the path down the cliff. I picked up a rhythm in my pace and breathing—a pace I could maintain without unduly straining muscles or my lungs. At this speed I could run long distances without becoming exhausted or disheartened. I saw the symbolism here in thoughts that floated through my mind.

Yet as I ran back down the beach my enthusiasm cooled. I felt alone again, desperately alone, with the loneliness that slithers to the side of men who have gone out by themselves and sought new frontiers. It is a loneliness that chills the sense of adventure, a loneliness that fosters fear, that gives grotesque shape to shadows, makes sinister the innocent sounds of night.

I did not know, not then, that Patty was up there on the cliff, watching me, praying for me, loving me. I did not understand that I was not alone—that none of us is ever totally alone.

Patty was to tell me later how her heart had gone out to me as she had watched me stride down the beach. "I spoke to you, Tommy," she told me. "I called your name and told you that I would always be with you, that we'd always be together no matter how far we're separated by time and space."

When I reached the cliff top and the road that turns toward our home, I was sweating from my physical exertion, yet fear and resentment had seized me once again—fear of being drawn back into the narrow, controlled world of my youth, resentment against Patty for reminding me of my responsibility to those other "Tommy Sullivans out there."

As I stepped off the curb I decided firmly that I would not accept the invitation from the Braille Institute, that I would not make that speech I had shouted into the off-sea wind. I smelled success, riches, acclaim. Let those other Tommy Sullivans claw and clutch their own way to salvation. Let them make it on their own or let them wallow and sink in their self-created bogs of terror and incompetence.

But in that moment fate played an unexpected card, heralded by a sudden screech of tires. A car swerved around the corner from the coastal road. In the split second that I was aware of danger, Heidi leaped at my chest and threw me backward. She had been trained to meet an emergency like this, disciplined to react instinctively to her master's peril.

As I rolled across the sidewalk, the car struck Heidi. I heard the sickening thud of metal hitting flesh, not my flesh but the flesh of a German shepherd, a dog unhesitatingly ready to sacrifice her life for mine.

The driver didn't stop. The sound of the engine faded and I heard Heidi's whimper as she fell beside me. I reached out and touched her flank, touched fur wet with blood.

Patty too had heard the scream of tires. She came running now and in a moment her arms were around me, her face pressed to mine, her heart thumping like a drum.

"I'm okay," I said. "It's Heidi. What's happened to Heidi?"

We carried bruised and bleeding Heidi to our home across the tree-lined street. Within the long hour when Patty and I waited for the diagnosis of the veterinary surgeon, I told Patty that I would talk to the blind at the Braille Insitute, meet and encourage anyone at any time who might be aided by learning of my own experience.

Heidi's wound was not fatal, although she took many painful weeks to recover from the accident. She lies at my feet as I review this chapter. As I lean down and stroke her ears, she thumps her tail into the carpet.

Heidi did what she was trained to do and did it gallantly. But she more than saved my life. She helped to change my life at the deepest level. She helped me understand that we are, each one of us, our brother's keeper.

I take no credit for this resolve. I had first to recognize that if an animal, a dog, is ready to sacrifice its life for a human being, how much more responsible is every human being for his fellow man.

15. Wood Burnings and Whispers

Patty and I were sitting on the flagstones beside the log fire in our living room. Her head was on my shoulder and she was reading aloud the first draft of the first chapter of this, my story. Suddenly she tilted her chin and asked, "What did you really mean when you told Blythe, 'If you could see what I hear'?"

I ran my fingers through her hair and replied, "Not only what I hear, but what I touch and smell and taste."

"Tell me," she said.

"It'll make it a long night."

"Some of the things."

I thought for a moment of my world of four senses, the only world I've known. I'm convinced that it is more exciting, more perceptive than the worlds of many sighted people. I do not undervalue sight, for sight has to be the most important of the senses. But, compelled to do so, I have been able to supersensitize the other faculties. I do not see a smile, for instance, but when the person who smiles speaks I can tell at once whether the smile is true or false. A flash of teeth can camouflage the heart; not so a voice.

"When you wake up in the morning, Patty, you see light. It makes no difference to me whether my eyelids are closed or open. But my first awareness is the smell of you."

She laughed. "What do I smell of?"

"Of you."

"Different from other people?"

"Quite unique." I grinned.

"Has everyone a different smell?"

"Of course. Animals understand this. How do you

176

think lambs find their mothers in a flock of sheep? How does a bloodhound track down a robber?"

"But you've got special gifts, Tommy."

"Sure. I'm a genius! Didn't my Dad tell you? Hell, I'm not saying that talents aren't handed out in different measures. What I'm sure of, though, is that if I can sharpen up the receptivity of my four senses, then anyone can. You can. Blythe can. Tommy can. People who don't develop all the senses are only half alive."

"Like listening to half an orchestra," mused Patty.

"Right," I said, "and in my orchestra the strings have been left out. But I can hear the woodwinds, the brass and percussion, and inside my head I can hear the missing strings."

"Like Beethoven did?"

"Something like Beethoven."

Patty leaned forward and threw another log on the fire. For a while I listened to the unseasoned wood crackling and spitting. Then she asked, "What do I smell of now?"

"From the sublime to perspiration," I declared. "From Eroica to erotica." I moved my hands. "Why not ask me about the sense of touch?"

"Do I have to?" She laughed. "I wonder how much Don Juan would have paid for your fingertips."

"Not for sale!"

"So long as you play like that only for me."

"Only for you," I assured her.

But as I explored the warmth of Patty I suddenly remembered the touch of Blythe's flesh when I had carried her unconscious from the pool. The contrast was incredible. With Blythe I had touched death—her flesh alabaster smooth, cold, yielding and without the scent of life.

Patty cut short memory of both the horror at the pool and the miracle of survival when she asked, "What else do you like to touch?"

I wrenched my thoughts away from recollection of Blythe's inert body and said, "Things like driftwood, the roughness of a rock—almost anything made by nature."

I told her how the feel of concrete and steel, for instance, gave me a sense of strength but they also spelled out brutality and aggression. Wood, on the other hand—a walnut tabletop or baseball bat—aroused in me a feeling of well-being, of man's activity and craftsmanship. I told her how I responded to nature's imperfections and unexpectedness.

My hand brushed a pine cone on the hearth and I invited Patty to feel its spikes and depressions, each subtly different from its neighbors. She asked about flowers and I reflected how they made me think not merely of petals and scent but of the seed and the thrust of the blade through soil.

"I want our children to understand the wholeness and rhythm in everything—to comprehend the origin of all things, the struggle for growth and evolution. I sometimes think that as a blind person I've been able to get closer to God the Creator than sighted people can.

"I don't know who God is, or what He wants or why He put us here. But there have been times when I seem to have been conscious of His presence. Would you call that faith?"

"Ask Father Bill," said Patty. "I'm not a theologian."

"But you've got something I often envy."

"Perhaps," said Patty, "more important than what you believe is how you live."

"Then why do you go to Mass every Sunday?"

"Because I need to," she said simply. "Maybe because I haven't got your strength." I knew she was smiling.

"When are you going to convert me?"

She tilted her head again and her breath was warm on my face. "You remember my telling you when we first met—on the beach at Hyannis Port—that you can't argue about faith? You either have it or you haven't."

"I'd like to have your faith."

"That's a change. You laughed at me once, remember?"

"I'm still laughing."

"Not so loudly."

"No." I nodded. "Not so loudly."

We didn't pursue the subject further. Not then. We spoke about prejudice, and I pointed out another advantage in being blind.

"When a sighted person sees something or someone, his brain makes an instant judgment—he's ugly, she's pretty, that's yellow or green or big or small. I can't do that. I can't see out there. My world is one of intimate confrontation, not of faraway or middle-distance images. I think I gain in not being able to make quick judgments. I have to concentrate more on everyone I meet. I have to allow the senses of smell, touch and sound to send their different evaluations to my mind. Only then can I judge a person's worth."

Patty asked me if I felt anything was ugly.

"Of course, there are foul smells like blocked drains and skunks and stale sweat. There are unpleasant tastes like aspirin and burned toast. I hate the sound of ambulances. Their sirens scream pain and fear. But I've truly never met an ugly person—not physically ugly. Old people with wrinkles and deformed people can be very beautiful to me. I don't see leathered skins and twisted limbs. I see inside them. An old voice often means experience and wisdom and tolerance. A callused hand means someone who has worked hard."

We talked of handshakes, and I told her how much they reveal of a person's mood and personality. The finger-touch handshake, for instance, meant that a person was not really interested in meeting you. The quick business handshake often meant that a person was interested only in exploiting a situation. The limp handshake revealed depression, moral defeat, shallowness of character, boredom.

"But the handshake of a friend ... Ah! That's quite different. The friend holds onto a hand an instant or two longer and he usually pumps his arm up and down. This handshake connotes warmth, gratitude, good humor or compassion. When a sighted person shakes a hand he looks at the expression of a face. But the face can lie. The face can be a mask. People forget the message that their hands reveal."

We talked of footsteps too—of how much is given away by the style of a walk: the shuffling steps of weary people and people tired of life; the free-spirit steps of children running; the hesitant steps of people without self-confidence; the firm, striding steps of those who know what they're about.

"People with sight," I said, "cannot look at anyone or anything for long without losing concentration. It's the other way around for me. My concentration builds up when I meet someone. My senses distill an essence. I'm not distracted by movement. I zero in on people and stay with them. Sight paints a picture of life, but sound, touch, taste and smell are actually life itself. Sometimes, Patty, I wish I didn't see so clearly."

"Sounds sort of scary," she protested.

"Why should knowing people, I mean really understanding people, be alarming?"

"Because everyone wants to hide a bit of himself," she said.

"Yet if we really knew each other, wouldn't we be more human? Wouldn't we have an answer to some of the things that divide us—like suspicion, fear, concealed motives and need?"

We let this thought hang in the warm air of the fireside until Patty said, "Tell me what you love best—your favorite things."

"Do you want me to sing that song out of *The Sound of Music*—you know, 'Brown paper packages tied up in string, raindrops and roses and whatever'?"

"Seriously," she said with a laugh.

The list I made was long enough for the fire to cool. I spoke of the obvious things I relished, like the whisper of wind in grass, and less obvious things like the appetizing smells of an apartment building in the early evening when twenty different dinners are being cooked. I tried to describe the sound of snow falling (who but the blind have taken the time to listen to the fall of snowflakes?). It was easier for Patty to understand my superlatives when I spoke of a choir in a great cathedral and the squeak of newly washed hair. Among the most sensuous sounds, I told her, was the caressing swish of nylon stockings when a woman walks. My list included the whoosh of a toboggan, the thunder of horses' hoofs and the exhilaration of a storm.

Then we sat for a while in the comfortable silence that lovers know. A sudden hiss from the dying fire broke up our reverie. We stretched and yawned, and because it was now dark it was I who led Patty to the bedroom of our children. We stood, side by side, listening to the steady breathing of Blythe and Tommy. Patty leaned down and puffed a pillow. Then she turned to Blythe and pulled up a rumpled blanket. Heidi joined us and nuzzled my legs. It was a scene enacted each evening in a million homes.

I took Heidi out for her evening walk. I heard her padding toward her favorite spot on the lawn. The air was champagne crisp. Suddenly from the house I heard Patty calling my name urgently.

"Tommy, quickly, quickly!"

I spun on my heel. She met me at the door, breathless with excitement.

"Listen," she panted. "Can't you hear it?"

"What?"

"Your new song. 'If You Could See What I Hear.' It's on the radio."

I have no idea what adventures, what triumphs and misfortunes lie ahead. I have no idea whether we will live in mansions or in attics, whether Patty will wear tiaras or faded ribbons. The excitement of the moment was not precariously balanced on a single achievement or upon the enthusiastic predictions of one disc jockey.

The moment had much deeper meaning than that. I was not so naïve as to believe that a few radio waves on the midnight air heralded a flood tide of success, that they signaled Everest had been conquered. I'm very conscious of being only twenty-six years old. If I am granted the allotted span, I know well enough that my journey will be milestoned by disappointments, by many setbacks.

The thought that overwhelmed my mind then, however, was of a small boy understanding for the first time that he had to battle his way through life with what some believed was the harshest handicap of all. I had proven to others, but more importantly to myself, that I could compete with anyone for whatever trophies upon which I might set my mind—and I could demonstrate to others that life's real rewards are truly in the striving.

It might be, I thought, that we who are handicapped, who are most severely challenged, are given blessings and the chance of winning treasure denied those many who are born without physical handicaps.

Ten minutes later, Patty was warmly encircled in my arms. Ecstasy peaked and curved downward to the plains of satiety and peace. A moment before we slept, she whispered, "I can see what you hear, Tommy."

"What do you see?"

"Love," said Patty softly—very softly.

Great Reading from SIGNET

☐ **ALAN ALDA: AN UNAUTHORIZED BIOGRAPHY by Jason Bonderoff.** (#AE1419—$2.75)*

☐ **FIRST YOU CRY by Betty Rollin.** (#AE1259—$2.50)

☐ **SAVE ME THE WALTZ by Zelda Fitzgerald.** (#Y5603—$1.25)

☐ **BOGIE by Joe Hyams.** (#E9189—$1.75)

☐ **KATE: THE LIFE OF KATHARINE HEPBURN by Charles Higham.** (#AE1212—$2.95)

☐ **PENTIMENTO by Lillian Hellman.** (#AE1543—$2.95)

☐ **ELEANOR: THE YEARS ALONE by Joseph P. Lash.**
(#AE1293—$3.95)

☐ **ELEANOR AND FRANKLIN by Joseph P. Lash.**
(#AE1231—$4.95)

☐ **SINATRA by Earl Wilson.** (#E7487—$2.25)

☐ **THE WOMAN HE LOVED by Ralph G. Martin.** (#E9074—$2.50)

☐ **THE ROCKEFELLERS by Keith Colher and David Horowitz.**
(#E8869—$2.95)

☐ **IF YOU COULD SEE WHAT I HEAR by Tom Sullivan and Derek Gill.** (#AE1240—$2.50)

☐ **SONG OF SOLOMON by Toni Morrison.** (#AE1446—$2.95)

☐ **THREE BY FLANNERY by Flannery O'Connor.**
(#E9792—$2.95)

☐ **KINFLICKS by Lisa Alther.** (#E9794—$2.95)

*Price slightly higher in Canada

Buy them at your local bookstore or use this convenient coupon for ordering.
THE NEW AMERICAN LIBRARY, INC.,
P.O. Box 999, Bergenfield, New Jersey 07621
Please send me the books I have checked above. I am enclosing $_____
(please add $1.00 to this order to cover postage and handling). Send check or money order—no cash or C.O.D.'s. Prices and numbers are subject to change without notice.
Name_____
Address_____
City _____ State _____ Zip Code _____
Allow 4-6 weeks for delivery.
This offer is subject to withdrawal without notice.